THE GAME OF
GO

THIS IS A CARLTON BOOK

Text, design and illustrations
copyright © Carlton Books Limited, 1998

2 4 6 8 10 9 7 5 3 1

A CIP catalogue for this book is available from the British Library.

ISBN 1 85868 491 9

PROJECT EDITOR: Roland Hall
DESIGNER: Mary Ryan
PRODUCTION: Sarah Schuman

Printed and bound in China

THE GAME OF
GO

LEARNING AND MASTERING
THE MOST CHALLENGING GAME
IN THE WORLD

Matthew Macfadyen

CARLTON

CONTENTS

HOW TO USE THIS BOOK

This book is intended as both an introduction to the game of Go for complete beginners and a guide to the principles of skilful play for players who have already mastered the rules.

At every stage of learning the game, the best way to understand new ideas is to try them out by actually playing. If you have a suitable opponent, the ideal way to begin is by playing the simplified versions of the game described in the first two chapters. It is strongly recommended that your first few games should be on a smaller board than the full 19 x 19 one.

If you prefer to see all the rules written down before you start learning the basics, or if you think you might already know them, look at page 34 first. There is also a small collection of problems summarizing the rules on page 35. If you prefer to absorb the general idea before dealing with specifics, play through the example game on pages 27–31.

Chapters 3 to 7 are concerned with various aspects of skilful play. These will be much easier to follow if you have already tried playing a few games, or if you know the game already. The problem sections at the ends of the chapters can be used both for revision and as an introduction to using the material in the chapter.

The example game in chapter 8 is probably best left until you have practiced enough on a small board to feel that you have a grasp of the basic tactics. It would make a good introduction to the full-sized board when you feel ready for the larger challenge.

When you have absorbed the rest of the book, the challenge problems in chapter 9 will introduce you to the wealth of possibilities in the game. These puzzles are not easy, and the solutions are not given.

A brief history of the game occupies much of chapter 10. The last few pages of the book introduce various ways to explore the game further, at Go clubs, through books and on the Internet.

CHAPTER ONE: CAPTURE

Go is a game of surrounding. Starting with an empty board, the two players try to spread their stones so as to surround as much of the board as possible, and the main method for achieving this is to surround the opponent's stones, or threaten to do so.

The elements of the game are simple. The board is marked with lines, and the pieces, called stones, are played on the lines. Here is a diagram of a small Go board, with 9 lines in each direction. The game is about half-way through.

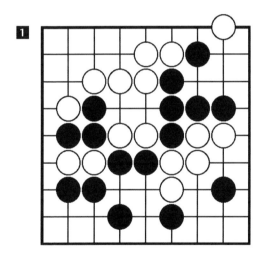

Notice that the stones are played on the lines, and can be played on the edge of the board. If you have not seen the game before, the patterns of stones here will look pretty random. Which side is surrounding what? The first step in understanding is to learn the process for capturing a single stone.

> *A stone surrounded completely by the opponent's stones is removed from the board.*

Capture is best explained by example. Here are some situations in which single stones can be captured. Black could occupy any of the four points marked x in diagram 2, and would then remove a white stone from the board, resulting in the positions shown in diagram 3.

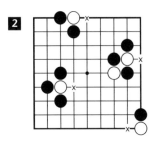 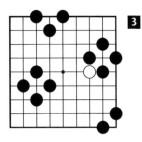

Notice that the edge is hostile to both sides, so that a stone on the edge can be captured by three enemies, and a stone in the corner by two. Notice also that diagonals do not count for this purpose, so that only four stones are needed to complete a capture in the centre, not eight.

Stones may be rescued from capture by connecting them along the lines to others of the same colour. But it is also possible to capture several stones at once, provided that all of the empty spaces around them are filled. Diagram 4 shows three chains of four white stones each of which can be captured. Black plays at x produce the positions in diagram 5.

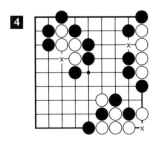 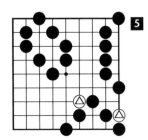

I n the lower right position in diagram 4, White was also in a position to do some capturing – do you see how? But the two stones marked with triangles in diagram 5 do not prevent White's four stones from being captured.

We are now ready to state the capture rule in full:

> *A chain of stones connected along the lines of the board is removed immediately when the last empty space adjacent to it is occupied by an opponent's stone.*

W e call these vital empty spaces Liberties. If a chain of stones itself surrounds some empty points, then those points are included with the liberties, so that the white chain in diagram 6 is not yet surrounded. Black can play at x however, and capture seven white stones, producing the position in diagram 7.

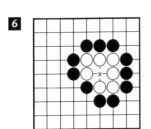
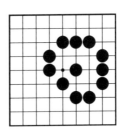

T he circumstances in which chains of stones can become permanently safe from capture are discussed in Chapter 3, starting on page 38, but the capture rule by itself produces an interesting game, and the rest of this chapter is devoted to Atari Go, the capturing game.

ATARI GO –
THE CAPTURING GAME

Atari means an immediate threat to capture. Some players like to warn their opponent of such a threat by saying "atari" when their opponent's chain of stones is reduced to one liberty.

Atari Go is a simplified version of the game in which the first player to capture a stone wins. This game is a good introduction to the tactical elements of Go, and one of the best ways to get a feel for the mechanics of the game is to find a friend and play a few dozen games of Atari Go.

Here are a pair of diagrams showing a game of Atari Go played on a 9 line board. The numbers indicate the order in which the stones are played. Black always plays first in Go. Diagram 9 shows the second half of the game; here the stones which were already played in diagram 8 have had their numbers removed, so that the new numbers are easier to find.

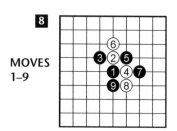

MOVES
1–9

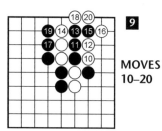

MOVES
10–20

In this game moves 5, 7, 10, 12, and 18 are all "atari" plays which threaten capture next turn. Each time the opponent defends by playing where the capture was threatened. Black 19 is also atari, but this time White has no need to defend since 20 captures four stones and White wins the game. Try some games with a friend. Do you do better by attacking opposing stones or by patiently defending your own weak spots and waiting?

TRICKS FOR CAPTURING STONES

The basic element of the capturing game is the exchange of Black's move 1 for white 2 in diagram 10. With move 1, Black plays "atari" and threatens to capture a white stone on the next move. To defend against this threat White plays at 2, expanding the threatened stone to become part of a two stone chain.

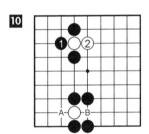

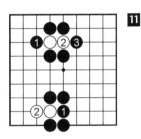

But move 2 expands the chain of white stones from having just one liberty to having three. Since Black can only occupy one liberty on each move, the white stones will normally escape unless there are some extra factors in Black's favour.

The position at the bottom of diagram 10 shows an example. Here Black has a choice of two ways to play atari, as either of the points A and B threaten White.

The correct approach is to play A, as shown at the top of diagram 11. Then White cannot escape effectively. If, on the other hand, Black plays B, as in the bottom position in diagram 11, White can escape (at least for the moment) with move 2.

Chasing your opponent's stones towards your own is the essence of capturing. The edge of the board is another good place to chase them.

SOME MORE TRICKS FOR CAPTURING STONES

D iagram 12 illustrates three different positions in which Black can get to force a capture. Diagram 13 shows how.

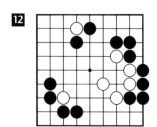

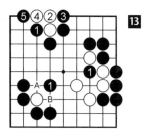

I n the top position, the white stone is quite close to the edge. Black's strategy here is to force the white chain towards the edge with move 1, then if White replies at 2 there is a choice of points at 3 and 4, either of which is atari and forces the capture as shown.

In the lower left position there are two directions in which White might escape, but Black has helpful stones waiting in both directions. Rather than try for an immediate capture by playing at A or B in diagram 13, Black can patiently play the looser move at 1. This is good enough to prevent both of the escaping possibilities. There are many cases in Go where it is more effective to attack from a distance like this.

In the position on the right White has formed a group of five stones but they are not yet completely connected together, and still form four separate chains. It is always worth having a good look at such formations in case you can find a point which will be atari on two chains of stones at once. Diagram 13 shows the double atari, leaving White with no time to defend against both threats.

USING THE EDGE OF THE BOARD AND THE CUT

H ere is a position in which Black has three opportunities to capture some stones by using the edge of the board:

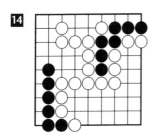

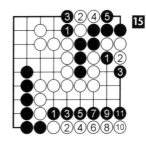

I n the top position, there is an odd stone which can be separated from the main white chain. Diagram 15 shows this separate chain being driven into the upper edge and surrounded.

To the right, White has two stones which are not properly connected. This time White can get as far as putting one of the black stones into atari (with 2) but it is too late, black 3 captures three stones.

The lower position shows a stone which can be cut off and chased along the edge of the board all the way to the corner.

Each of these positions, as well as illustrating the use of the edge of the board to help in capturing, shows Black using a cut. The black stones labelled 1 here all separate two white chains by playing on a point at which White could have connected them.

There is always a danger in playing on these 'cutting points' in Atari Go, since the cutting stone already has two of its four liberties occupied by enemy stones. Usually a cut results in one side or the other being captured quite quickly.

SURROUNDING AT A DISTANCE

This position looks quite promising for Black. The white stones are separated into several small chains while the long black chain in the centre has almost surrounded several of them.

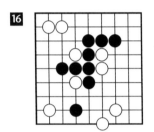

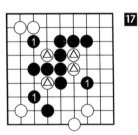

Diagram 17 shows three good moves from which Black could choose. We have seen the one in the upper left already. Note that the two odd white stones in the corner are not close enough to help rescue the stone marked with a triangle.

The other two black moves are a little looser, but in neither case can White escape. The common theme here is that the endangered white positions are already surrounded on two sides, and can only run out into empty space in one general direction. By playing a stone near the middle of the direction in which White will have to run away, Black reduces the options to squeezing through one of two very narrow gaps.

In these examples the gaps are just a little bit too small to fit through, though it may not be clear at first that the triangled stones in diagram 17 are unable to escape. Set the examples up on the board and experiment with different combinations by which White might try to escape.

SETTING UP THE DOUBLE ATARI

Diagram 18 shows a position in which two black stones have been surrounded by a loose ring of opposing stones as in our previous example, but now the surrounding net is just a little looser, and Black can escape.

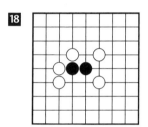

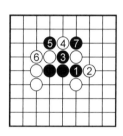

Pushing out through the gaps with moves 1 and 3 in diagram 19 leaves five points at which the white stones can be cut into separate chains. Then Black can play moves 5 and 7 in either order, the result will be a double atari, ensuring that one white stone will be captured. Note that the main black chain still has two liberties in the centre, so White cannot make a capture first.

If White succeeds in recognizing that the ring of stones is too weak to successfully contain Black, then one of moves 2 or 4 should be played defensively. Substituting white 2 for a stone at point 3 would be safer, but then Black could escape.

For Black, it is a good idea to test White's response by playing at 1 and 3 first before risking the cutting stones at 5 and 7. That way there will only be one black chain to look after if White should back down from trying to surround the black chain.

THE LADDER

If a chain of stones is running away straight along the lines of the board, it will normally be able to form extra liberties much faster than the opponent can fill them in, but there is a special case in which a stone is trying to escape crabwise, along a diagonal, and cannot break free so easily. Diagram 20 shows the starting position, and diagram 21 shows the trick:

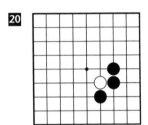 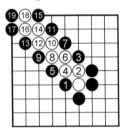

By playing atari on alternate sides of the white chain, Black is able to keep the pursuit hot. Whether the white stones can actually be captured depends on where the "ladder" is aiming. In diagram 21 it hits the side of the board, and White is captured.

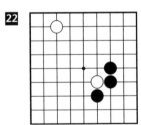 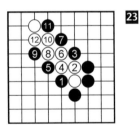

But if there is a white stone in the way, as in diagram 22, then the white chain gains an extra liberty with 12 in diagram 23 and Black has no continuation. This is a disaster for Black since White now has four different ways to play double atari.

SOME TRICKS FOR RESCUING STONES

If your chain of stones is under threat of immediate capture, there is no choice but to extend out into the widest space you can find. This at least gives you time to start some attacking of your own.

When the threat is not yet immediate though, you can play more safely. It is a good idea to forestall the danger of an attack by keeping your chains of stones connected together, or at least possible to connect.

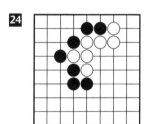

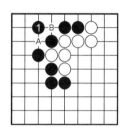

In diagram 24, for example, Black has four separate chains of stones, while White has only one. Black is in considerable danger of having some of the chains separated by cutting moves which would end up making a capture.

There are several different ways of achieving an effective connection. One of the most efficient of these is shown in diagram 25. The stone at 1 does not absolutely connect the black chains, but White is unable to play at either of the two cutting points A and B, since Black would be able to capture the cutting stone immediately.

As we introduce more of the complete game of Go, it will become apparent that efficiency is a prime objective. Using one stone to do two jobs, in the way that black 1 does here, is a good example of the efficient use of stones.

MORE CONNECTIONS

H ere are some more examples of ways to connect stones together. It is possible here to take full advantage of the fact that your opponent only gets to play one stone at a time.

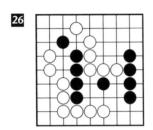

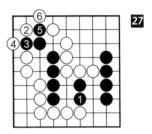

I n diagram 26, Black is in immediate danger of being separated into two chains, but the move at 1 in diagram 27 skilfully connects all the black stones together. Although the connection is not yet complete, Black retains two different ways to connect to each side, and since White only gets one move at a time, Black can guarantee a connection. This formation is known as the "Bamboo Joint".

Then White has a connecting move at 2. This may look pretty weak when Black pushes through at 3 and 5, separating the white stones into six different chains, but the formation is in the corner, and all of the cutting points which Black might want to play are protected by the edge of the board so that White would be able to capture any cutting stones immediately.

Connecting stones together and running out into the centre are good ways to prolong survival, but indefinite survival can be achieved only by a third type of defensive strategy – forming some liberties inside the chain of stones which are safe from enemy approach, known as eyes. The ways in which this can be achieved are discussed later, starting on page 38.

PROBLEMS

Here are some problems for you to try. In each position Black is to play, and the objective is to be the first to capture at least one stone. Some of these introduce new tricks, and some revise ones we have already looked at.

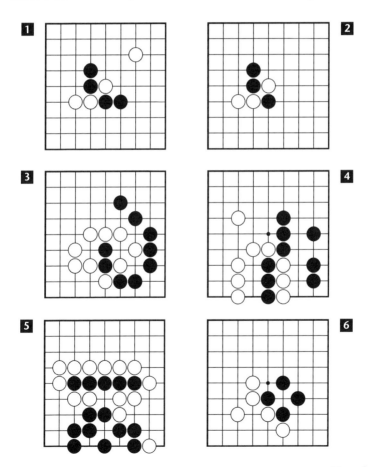

SOLUTIONS TO PROBLEMS

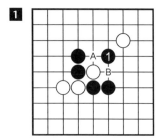

Black 1 encloses the central white stone in a loose net from which there is no escape. If Black is in too much of a hurry, and threatens the stone with immediate capture by playing A or B, then White can take the other one of those points and escape.

This is an example of the ladder. Black can threaten the white stones alternately from one side and the other and drive them across the board. When the ladder reaches the edge, White is captured. Note that this technique will fail if there is a white stone in the way, as in problem 1.

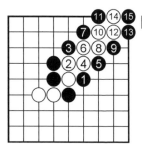

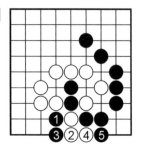

There is a loose white stone on the lower side which is not properly connected to its fellows. Black 1 in the diagram separates this stone and drives it towards the edge. Black 3 can also be played at 4, as White will be captured either way.

4

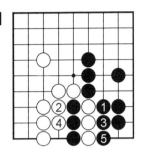

*B*oth sides have a group of three stones in danger on the lower edge. Victory will go to the first one to capture. Black must immediately start playing on the liberties of the three white stones, though 1, 3 and 5 here can be played in any order.

*B*lack has several ways to capture some white stones, but none of them are as fast as White's threat on the five stones in the centre. Black must first rescue those stones by playing at 1 in the diagram. Next move there will still be something to capture since Black has good moves at A, B and C.

5

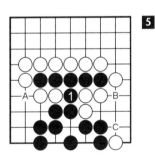

5

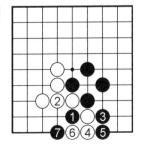

*B*lack 1 threatens to capture one stone by playing at 2 and separates another one at the same time. Then Black 3 creates the same shape we saw in problem 3, driving the stone towards the edge where it can be surrounded. Again Black has a choice at 5. This stone could be played at 6 instead.

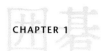

ETIQUETTE

Any activity as old as the game of Go develops traditions of behaviour associated with it. These are not really necessary to play the game, but it is good to know what to expect when you meet other players. Here are a few of the basics.

PLAYING THE STONES Do not pick up a stone until you have decided where to play, then hold the stone between the first two fingertips of your right hand, with the middle finger on top. With practice it becomes possible to slap the stone down quite forcefully onto the board. This is regarded as acceptably assertive rather than rude.

KEEPING THE PRISONERS If you capture some stones, remove them from the board and keep them in the lid of your stone container. Traditional sets have round wooden bowls to contain the stones, and the saucer-shaped lids are ideal for this purpose.

SAYING "ATARI" This is a slightly difficult one. Some players regard it as polite to warn their opponent that a capture is imminent. Some regard it as rude to suggest that so obvious a thing might not have been noticed. When playing Atari Go, and for your first few exploratory games, it is a good idea to say "atari" when you threaten a stone.

STARTING THE GAME Unless you start the game by playing on the centre point of the board, there will be a choice of which corner to occupy first. Traditionally this should be your upper right corner, and you should not play in your upper left corner (your opponent's near right) until the position has become unsymmetrical enough that this is a genuinely different place to play.

CHAPTER TWO: TERRITORY

I f you have experimented a little with the "Atari Go" game described in the previous chapter you have discovered that the 'running away' move, shown as white 2 in diagram 1, is an effective way to defend a stone unless White is running towards the edge of the board or towards more black stones.

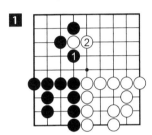

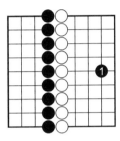

B ut when one side has a huge majority of stones in an area it is quite easy to capture anything which the opponent tries to play there. The lower half of diagram 1 is divided into a black area on the left and a white area on the right. Neither side can play on the spaces enclosed by the other's chain of stones without expecting to be captured rather soon.

The board will usually be divided into 'Spheres of influence' of this type, and during a game of Go there will normally be areas in which each side is pretty confident of capturing any enemy stone which is played there. The degree of confidence will vary with your experience. In diagram 2 for example there is no simple argument to show whether Black's stone at 1 is doomed or not. This brings us to the concept of territory:

> ***Your Territory consists of all those points on which you would expect to capture any stone the opponent played.***

Notice that as this definition depends on the expectations of the players, there is no absolute definition of territory.

THE TERRITORY GAME

W e will return later to the question of distinguishing areas which are secure territory from those which can be successfully invaded, but for the moment let us bypass the problem by introducing another simplified game: the Territory Game. For the purposes of the Territory Game, the rule is that you are only allowed to have one chain of stones on the board, and the objective is to form a chain which encloses the largest possible empty space.

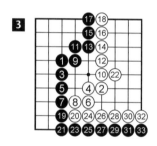

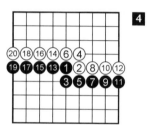

A game might look something like diagram 3. Play continues until both sides have finished walling off their territory, and then the territories are counted and compared.

At the end of diagram 3, Black has walled off 23 empty points, while White has 21 and four are neutral (count for yourself and check this). Black wins the game by two points.

It is not worth spending very long on this rather limited game. Three or four quick games with a friend may suffice to discover how it works. But it serves to introduce the idea of territory, and such principles of skilful play as it requires all apply to the full game with rather little adjustment. Some of the most important of these are listed on the next page:

PRINCIPLES OF THE TERRITORY GAME

The main lessons to learn from the Territory Game are:

◆ The game is counted by comparing the empty intersections surrounded by the two sides. The difference becomes the margin of victory.

◆ There will often be a neutral area in between the two sides' territories, and there is no particular purpose in playing there.

◆ It is more effective to play near the junction of the two sides' positions than inside your own area.

◆ Turning round the end of the opponent's chain (as at 5 and 6 in diagram 4) is a powerful manoeuvre which pushes the balance of the game in your favour.

◆ Once the chains of stones reach the edge, there is no advantage in playing further stones inside your own area; these only reduce your territory.

◆ The territories are not complete until the last stone is added at the edge of the board (11, 12, 19, 20 in diagram 4).

◆ When both sides are extending their chains in parallel, each is adding territory; the side whose chain is farther from the edge is building more territory.

◆ Even a small gap on the edge allows the opponent to encroach a long way into your territory (so White's move 22 in diagram 3 was a bad mistake, allowing Black to creep along the lower edge).

You may soon discover that the best moves for both sides produce a rather uninteresting pattern. If so, it is probably time to progress to the complete game of Go. Alternatively, you may enjoy exploring this game a little longer by insisting that the players start by playing at the edge of the board, or in the corners.

COMBINING THE SIMPLE GAMES

We are now ready to combine the principles of capture and territory to describe the game of Go. The players are free to occupy any empty point, stones may be captured but that does not end the game, and the size of the territories at the end of the game determines the winner. Adding a few definitions allows us to write the main rules of the game:

START The game begins with the board empty. Black plays first and then the players take turns to play a stone on any empty intersection.

CAPTURE If a play occupies the only liberty of a chain of the opponent's stones, those stones are removed from the board. The player making the capture retains the captured stones for counting purposes.

END Play continues until neither side can see anything useful to do. This is indicated by passing. When both players pass in succession the game stops.

TERRITORY Each player scores one point for every empty intersection surrounded by their stones, plus one point for each stone captured during the game. The winner is the player with the larger territory.

Essentially, that is it. We will need to add two more rules, one to help tidy the game up at the end and one to prevent positions from repeating themselves. The first of these is best described by looking at an example game, played on a nine-line board, and watching what happens at the end of the game. The problem of repeating positions is discussed on page 32.

AN EXAMPLE GAME

A game of Go typically starts with each side sketching out loose positions, trying to claim as much of the board as possible. Then there is a phase of skirmishing, in which the players contest each others' claims to the areas staked out.

5

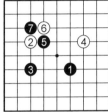

MOVES 1–7

This game starts with each side beginning a loose claim to two of the corners. The fighting begins with moves 6 and 7, which are both looking for ways to start the process of capturing something.

6

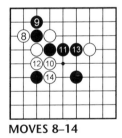

MOVES 8–14

White elects to abandon the stone at 6 for the moment, but makes good use of it by playing atari at 8 and 10. These two stones help to build a position in the lower left area.

Black 13 then tries to do several jobs at once: further isolating white 6 from safety, preparing an attack on white 4 and preparing to connect to black 1 in the lower right.

Now White decides to abandon the stone at 4 as well, and plays at 14 in an attempt to surround a large area in the lower left, including the capture of Black's stone 3. Both players are busily trying to do as many things at once as possible. The standard of play here is extremely high, so do not worry if the details seem mysterious to you at first. Just follow the flow of the game to see what happens, and come back for another look at it after you have played some games of your own.

THE GAME CONTINUES, MOVES 15–33

Black 15 isolates the white stone above it. White responds by feinting to rescue it with 16, but decides that these stones are doomed, and plays the clever combination of 18 and 20, expanding the lower left area to include both corners at the bottom of the board.

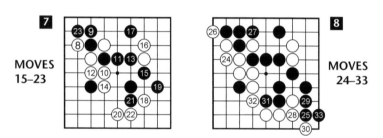

7

MOVES 15–23

8

MOVES 24–33

The territories are now essentially spoken for, and it remains only to argue about where exactly the boundaries will come. The following plays involve a number of threats to capture stones, and moves 24, 27 and 28 are all necessary defensive measures.

Black's move 25 is a clever way to make the most of the corner. White will have to connect up at 28, and so Black is able to expand into the corner with 29.

First, though, White slips in a stone at 26. This threatens to play at 27, which would rescue one white stone, capture three black ones and make a huge reduction in the black territory. This threat is unbearable for Black, who has to answer at 27. Only then does White return to the lower right area and connect at 28. This sort of switching back and forth between two (or more) areas of activity is typical of Go being played well.

The ability to judge which are the most important areas of the board depends mainly on long experience of the ways in which positions develop.

MOVES 34–50

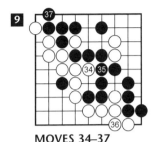

MOVES 34–37

The moves to 37 complete the boundaries of the two sides' territories, except for some neutral points which cannot be claimed by either player. But there is nothing to prevent play from continuing if either of the players thinks there is still anything to do; the game only ends when both players pass.

White continues as in diagram 10 in this instance, adding some extra stones to the two previously abandoned in the upper right, in black territory. The result creates a separate white territory containing two points, and if Black does not know what to do next this will have been a highly successful sequence for White.

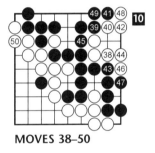

MOVES 38–50

An important principle here is that territory is only defined by the players' view of what can be captured, so a position which would be regarded as secure territory between one pair of players might be fiercely contested by another.

Similarly, a group of stones which one player may abandon as not worth trying to rescue might be regarded as secure in another game between different players. On the whole it is normal for more experienced players to abandon their stones rather earlier, experience telling them that certain positions are likely to be untenable.

See if you can find a way to capture the white stones before turning the page.

THE WHITE STONES CAPTURED

D iagrams 11 and 12 show how it is done. We have not discussed sacrifice tactics so far. They do not exist in the game of Atari Go, where the first capture ends the game.

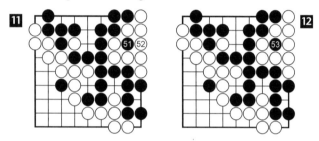

B lack adds a stone at 51 in diagram 11. This reduces the white formation in the area to one liberty, so that if White does nothing Black could continue by playing at 52, capturing a three stone chain and a five stone chain simultaneously.

But if White plays at 52, which captures the single stone 51 and connects all the white stones in the area into one chain of nine stones, then the entire White chain has only the one liberty at 53. Black can now play back onto that point, reducing White to no liberties and capturing the nine stone chain.

We will meet a number of other ways in which sacrifice stones can be used to reduce the opponent's options, but this pattern is one of the most common and important.

There is nothing to stop Black from having a similar try at rescuing the stone which has been abandoned in the lower left area, but here the players now decide that there is nothing worthwhile to do. The diagrams on the next page show the tidying up process by which the game is completed and counted.

COUNTING THE SCORE

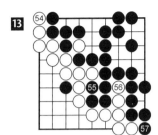

NEUTRAL POINTS First, fill in the neutral points, if there are any. Diagram 13 shows this process. Normally, the neutral points should be played as part of the game, with the players continuing to add stones alternately.

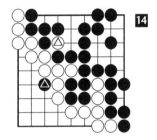

CLEANING Next, any stones which have been abandoned are removed and added to the stones captured during the game. There are two such stones in our game, they are marked with triangles in diagram 14.

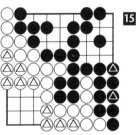

REPLACING PRISONERS Captured stones are worth one point each, and can conveniently be cancelled out using the opponent's territory, making the shapes easier to count in the process. In this game the 10 prisoners which Black captured, and White's two, are filled into the territories as shown in diagram 15.

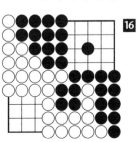

REARRANGING The Black territory is still a rather messy shape. Stones can be pushed around inside the territory to square it up a bit, as in diagram 16.

The result is that Black has 15 points to White's 9, or, adding captures to territory, a score of 27 to 21. Black wins by six points.

REPEATING POSITIONS – A CURIOSITY

The addition of the Cleaning rule, allowing helpless stones to be removed as prisoners during the counting phase, almost completes the rules of Go.

But there is a problem with the pattern shown in diagram 17. Here Black can capture one white stone, but the resulting shape will be just like the starting position, except that now White can capture one black stone.

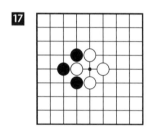

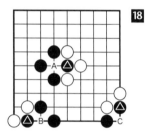

Diagram 18 shows the position after Black has captured, as well as two related shapes – on the side and in the corner.

If there were no special rule, these patterns could produce an endless repetition of the same position. The Japanese name for these shapes is Ko, which means 'Eternity'.

The rule is that you are only allowed to recapture after at least one intervening move elsewhere. There are several ways in which the exact ruling can be expressed. Here we will use a practical version:

> **When one stone is captured in the Ko formation, it is forbidden to recapture without an intervening play.**

"The Ko formation" refers to all of the three patterns shown in diagram 18, as well as more complex versions.

IMPLICATIONS OF THE KO RULE

M̲ost games involve examples of Ko. Sometimes it is just a matter of one stone, but often something like diagram 19 comes up. Here white 1 is a Ko capture, and White desperately wants to connect at the point above 1 to rescue the five marked stones in the upper left corner.

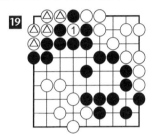

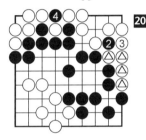

T̲he Ko rule prevents immediate recapture, but Black wants to do so as soon as it is allowed. The standard strategy is for Black to make a move elsewhere which threatens to do some damage. In this case there is an excellent candidate at 2 in diagram 20. Normally this would be pointless, since White can capture 2 with 3, but black 2 is atari on the four marked stones. If White answers at 2, then Black is allowed to recapture the Ko at 4 and now White needs a threat to keep Black busy for one move.

A̲lternatively, White may choose to connect the Ko, playing at 3 in diagram 21, and let Black capture the chain of four stones on the right as shown.

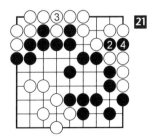

The possibility of apparently secure positions being destroyed in this way provides much of the richness in the game of Go.

THE RULES IN FULL

The complete rules then are:

START The game begins with the board empty. Black plays first and then the players take turns to play a stone on any empty intersection.

CAPTURE If a play occupies the only liberty of a chain of the opponent's stones, those stones are removed from the board. The player making the capture retains the captured stones for scoring.

KO When a stone is captured in the Ko formation, it is forbidden to recapture without an intervening play.

END Play continues until neither side can see anything useful to do. This is indicated by passing. When both players pass in succession the game stops.

CLEANING At the end of the game, any remaining neutral points are filled, then any stones which cannot be saved are removed from the board and added to the captured stones.

TERRITORY Each player scores one point for every empty intersection surrounded by their stones, plus one point for each stone they captured during the game. The winner is the player with the larger score.

HANDICAPS The advantage of playing first is offset by adding a number of points (usually 5½) to White's score at the end. Between players of different ranks, Black instead starts by playing a fixed number of free moves.

There is one common addition to these rules, which allows for games to be handicapped by player skill. This is discussed later on page 119.

PROBLEMS SUMMARISING THE RULES

1

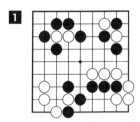

How many chains of stones does White have? Which of them can Black capture?

2

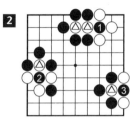

Is White allowed to recapture any of the stones 1, 2 and 3 immediately?

3

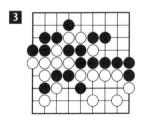

The game is almost over. What unfinished business needs to be resolved?

4

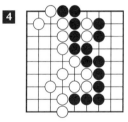

Black is about to play the last point of the game. Where is it? What is the result?

5

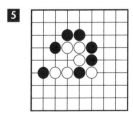

How can Black capture some stones?

6

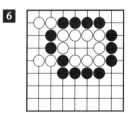

How can Black capture some stones?

SOLUTIONS TO PROBLEMS

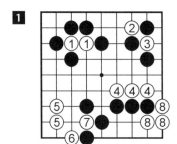

1

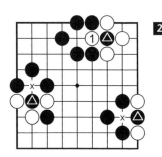

White has eight chains of stones. Of these, the ones numbered 1, 3 and 7 here can be captured immediately.

White is allowed to recapture immediately in the top position at 1. This does not repeat the previous position since Black captured two white stones with the marked play. But White is forbidden by the Ko rule from recapturing at either of the x points until there has been a move played elsewhere.

2

3

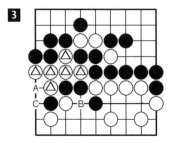

The six marked white stones are in atari. Black can capture them by playing A. White can rescue them by capturing two stones with B or capturing one stone with C. The white stones at the top cannot escape, so there is no hurry to capture them.

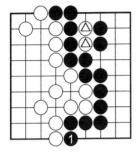

B lack completes the boundaries by playing at 1, and the game is over. The two white stones marked with triangles cannot be saved, and so are taken off as prisoners. Then Black has 25 points of territory plus two prisoners, making 27. White also has 27 points, so the game ends in a tie.

B lack's move 1 here fills the last liberty of the three marked stones, which should then be removed from the board and kept separately until the end of the game.

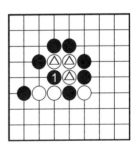

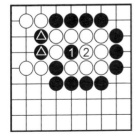

B lack must sacrifice a stone, starting either at 1 or 2. Then if White captures the sacrifice stone as shown Black can play on the same point again, capturing 10 stones; and if instead White plays elsewhere (for example threatening the two marked stones) Black can continue at 2 and capture 9 stones in the centre.

CHAPTER THREE:
LIFE AND DEATH

THE INSIDE BOUNDARY

The rules of Go tell us when a chain of stones has been captured and should be removed from the board and added to the collection of captured stones, but further investigation is necessary to discover which formations of stones are vulnerable to capture, and which are safe.

The key to this question is the inside boundary. The chain of white stones shown in diagram 1 is not yet captured, since it has a liberty at the point marked x. But Black can play at x, occupying the last liberty, and capture the white stones.

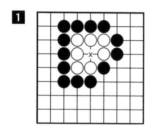 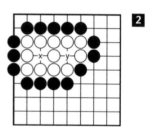

In diagram 2, by contrast, the white chain has two separate spaces inside it. Now Black has no way to capture the stones. A play at either x or y would be insufficient to fill all of White's liberties, and a black stone at either of these points would itself be surrounded and removed.

These points inside the boundary of a chain of stones are known as eyes. A group of stones which has formed, or is able to form two separate eyes cannot be captured. Such groups are referred to as "alive". By contrast, stones which are unable to form two eyes or connect up to other living stones are "dead".

If the fate of a group of stones is undecided, and depends on which side gets to play first, they are described as "unsettled".

CHAINS AND GROUPS

So far we have mainly been concerned with chains of stones, clusters which are solidly connected along the lines of the board, and which can only be captured as a unit. When looking at the life and death of formations it is often more useful to refer to groups of stones, loose clusters which have not yet finished connecting up, but which are likely to be able to do so.

Diagram 3 shows a position in which White has four groups of stones, two consisting of one chain and two of three. Black has one group consisting of three chains. The black group has plenty of ways to connect its chains together, and can make eyes in several ways by doing so. It is quite safe, but the white groups are not all secure. See if you can identify the dead white group.

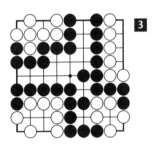

The upper left group is the most obviously secure. It has only one chain of stones, and has already formed two separate eyes.

The upper right group has only one chain of stones, but the space inside is not yet divided into two eyes. However there are two ways to do this. White will be able to play at least one of the points 1 and 2 in diagram 4, and since either of these suffices to divide the space in two the group cannot be killed.

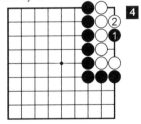

The lower left group is also safe. It has two separate eyes, and although there are three chains of white stones there is no way for Black to capture one of them separately.

FALSE EYES

The white group in the lower right is not secure. It has two separate eyes, but there are three chains of stones, and the outer chain of three stones can be captured separately from the others.

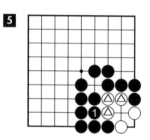

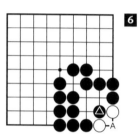

Black can play atari on three stones with move 1 in diagram 5, and White has no defence. Connecting the stones together would mean filling in White's own liberty, allowing Black to capture six stones by playing at the corner point. If White does not reply though, then the marked black stone in diagram 6 captures three stones and puts the other two into atari.

The shape White has here is known as a False Eye. Its characteristic feature is that the chains of stones either side of the false eye are not connected in any other way. Diagram 7 shows some more examples of false eyes. The large white group there is dead. It has only one eye (can you see where?) but all of the other spaces surrounded by white stones are false eyes. Black can fill the remaining outside liberties and then capture the group one chain at a time, starting with a Ko capture such as the one already available in the lower right corner.

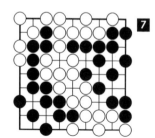

CREATING FALSE EYES BY SACRIFICING STONES

The white formation in diagram 8 is on the way to making two eyes but the space on the right is vulnerable. Black can steal the eye there with a sacrifice at 1 in diagram 9. If White captures, then the resulting space will be a false eye. To make a real eye White needs to play at the point 1.

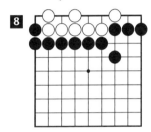

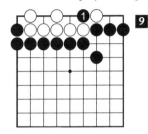

Quite often, a sacrifice move which steals an eye in this way will be atari, so that the threat forces the opponent to answer locally and it is possible to play a second attacking move. Diagram 10 shows an example. White appears at first to have plenty of ways to form eyes, but black 1 in diagram 11 threatens to capture the marked stone. If White replies by capturing the stone as shown, there is time to play another eye-stealing move at 3 and kill all of the white stones.

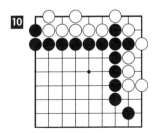

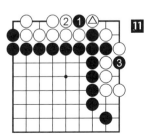

MORE SACRIFICE TRICKS

We have already met the trick for capturing the white group in diagram 12. This two-point eye can be reduced to a one point eye (or captured next move anyway) by playing the sacrifice stone at 1 in diagram 13.

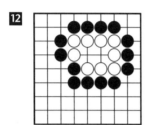

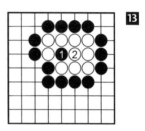

This process can be extended, provided that the shape of the eye is simple enough. The white groups in diagram 14 illustrate how a four-point eye can be progressively eroded by sacrificing stones inside it.

White is helpless during this process, except that it takes rather a large number of moves for Black to complete the process of capturing the white stones. This means that any counterattack on the surrounding black groups has plenty of time to be pursued to a conclusion.

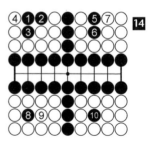

The key to Black's technique is that at every stage the black sacrifice stones themselves form a compact shape which, when captured, will not be able to be divided into two separate spaces. There are only a small number of shapes compact enough for this to work. They are shown on the next page.

D iagram 15 shows all of the nine shapes of stones which are compact enough to be reduced to a single eye by progressive sacrifice of the type we are discussing. If a group of stones has only one area of territory inside it, and that area is in one of these shapes, then the opponent can play in the middle of the shape and eventually capture the group by using sacrifice.

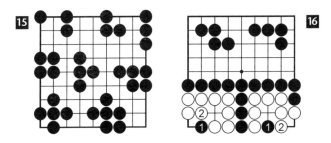

T wo shapes which are not in the collection are shown at the top of diagram 16. White groups surrounding these shapes are illustrated at the bottom of the diagram, where Black's attempts to reduce the shape fail.

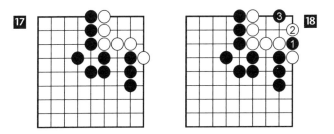

D iagram 17 shows a small white corner which can be killed using these techniques. Black starts with a sacrifice on the edge at 1 in diagram 18. This stone is captured by white 2 but only produces a false eye. The remaining space has now been reduced to one of the dead shapes, and black 3 keeps it that way.

HOW TO KILL

During a game of Go, we are interested not just in taking opportunities to kill the opponents' stones, but also in knowing where we are likely to be able to kill any invader. This is what is meant by territory.

Suppose that the position in diagram 19 arises, We are Black, and hope that our large territory of 34 points is secure. Certainly it is bigger than White's 25-point area at the bottom. But what if White attempts to build a new group of stones in our area with 1 in the diagram?

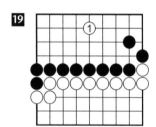
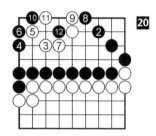

The basic method here is to start by restricting the amount of space available for White to form eyes, and then look at the shape of the space remaining and play a stone in the centre of it if necessary.

Here we might start at 2 in diagram 20. Then if White tries to surround some space as shown, we creep in from both sides with 4, 6, 8 and 10 to reduce the space.

It is important to notice that, although the stone 10 is in atari, White would only make a false eye by capturing it. This means that we have time to play in the centre of the white eye at 12. Now White has no way to make two eyes, and can only hope to rescue the invading group by mounting an attack on the entire black formation. But we carefully began to attack with 2, making space for our own eyes in the upper right corner while attacking, so the black group is safe and the white one is going to die.

SMALL CORNERS

The corner of the board is much the easiest place to form living groups of stones quickly. There are already two edges to help in making the surrounding wall. The edge of the board is the next easiest place to live, and in the centre it is quite difficult to form secure eyes. As you practise playing the game, a number of the common patterns of stones and their properties will become familiar to you. It is very useful to have some reference positions with which to compare.

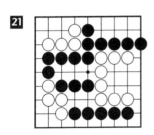

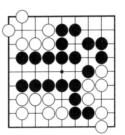

Here are some. The three groups of white stones in diagram 21 are all dead, provided both sides play accurately. The three in diagram 22 are all alive without requiring any extra defensive play.

It takes a considerable amount of study to be sure of these results. If you like that sort of challenge then experimenting with these shapes would be a good place to start. Otherwise, just have a look at these two diagrams to see roughly how big a group of stones has to be to be able to survive.

Notice that the living groups are slightly larger and knobblier than the dead ones. On the whole it is much easier to divide an irregular shape into two parts than a roundish one. The progressive sacrifice method involves playing in the middle of a space, and knobbly spaces with no obvious middle are usually alive.

CAPTURING TWO STONES MAKES A FALSE EYE

Our basic method for killing stones – eroding space from the outside and playing in the centre if needed – can often be speeded up: an eye cannot be formed by capturing two stones on the edge of the board.

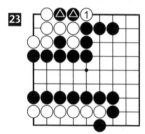 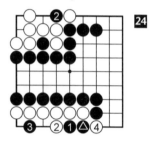

Diagram 23 shows the basic pattern. White captures the two marked stones with move 1, but Black can then reply by throwing in a stone at 2 in diagram 24. There is not much point in capturing this stone, since White would only make a false eye by doing so. The bottom of diagram 23 shows how to apply this to force false eyes.

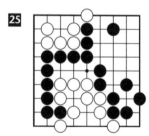 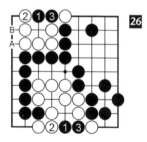

Here are two more versions of this idea. White's healthy-looking groups in diagram 25 can be killed by offering two-stone captures (White's alternate move 2 in the upper area – at 3 – is beaten by A, B, 2).

LIFE AND DEATH PROBLEMS

I t is Black's turn in all of these positions. In the first four problems Black's task is to kill the white stones; in problems 5 and 6 Black is asked to rescue the isolated group in the corner.

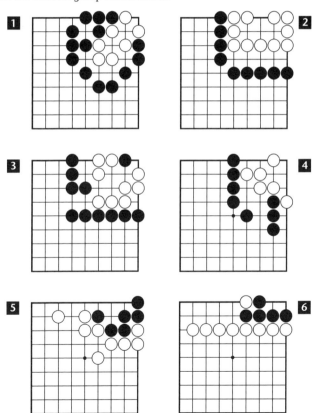

CHAPTER 3

SOLUTIONS TO PROBLEMS

1

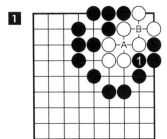

Black 1 makes sure that White only has a false eye at A, and B was already a false eye so the diagram leaves Black able to capture the group in three separate pieces. If White gets to play at 1 the group will be secure, and Black would then have no way to play atari.

Black 1 is the vital point, enabling Black to kill the group by the progressive sacrifice method. A white stone at 1 would divide the space into three separate eyes and make it completely secure.

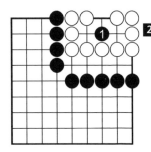

2

3

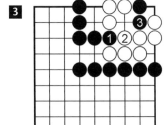

First, Black must reduce the space available inside the white group by pushing in with 1. Then Black 3 makes sure that the remaining space is only worth one eye. If Black had started at 3, White could reply at 1 and the space would be too large for the progressive sacrifice method to work.

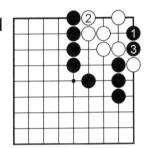

Black 1 reduces the space on the right to at most one eye, and also makes a double threat: to take away the eye on the right as shown, or to take the other one by playing at 2. Either way White ends up with only one eye and is dead.

Black 1 is the only way to divide the rather small space available into two separate eyes. A black play at A would fail, since White could then play at 1 and kill the group by making progressive sacrifices.

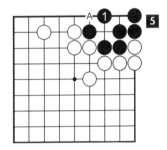

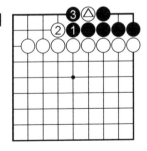

Black must start by expanding the available space with 1. Then the marked stone can be captured to make an eye. If Black is in too much of a hurry to capture, and starts by playing at 3, White can take the important point at 1 and Black only gets a false eye at the marked point.

CHAPTER FOUR:
THE FULL-SIZED BOARD

The full-sized, 19-line board seems to be very large at first sight. If you just learn the capturing rule and start playing it is hard to imagine what to do with all that space, and the action will probably creep around the board, with each move trying to capture the opponent's last stone, or else to rescue the stone it was attacking.

If you have not played the game before, it is a good idea to play a few games on a smaller board. You can use one designed for the purpose, or just shrink a full board by dividing off a corner, laying two pieces of paper on it to give you a section of 9 lines each way.

Once you have got the hang of some of the basic tactics it becomes much easier to follow what is going on across the whole board, and your games should increasingly involve ignoring your opponent's moves in order to take the chance to have first shot at a new area.

The easiest place to form secure territory is near the corners of the board, and the most straightforward way to play is for both sides to claim a share of the corners early on.

A very important strategic point is that it is normally a bad idea to form a group of stones which is only just alive at the beginning of the game. We will return to this point in the discussion of invasions in the next chapter. For the moment let us follow the implication; since your opponent has better things to do than contest areas which you have almost secured, there is no great hurry to secure your positions absolutely.

In practice this means that it is not worth playing right on the edge, and most commonly the first moves of the game are three or four lines out from the side. For these purposes we count the very edge of the board as the first line, so the little spots are counted as being on the fourth line. The recommended starting moves are on the line with the spots, or one line closer to the edge than that.

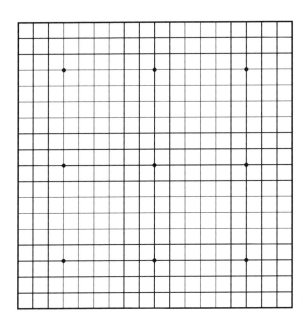

THE FULL-SIZED BOARD.

The little dots are used mostly to help your orientation. They are called "star points".

1

Since the corners are the easiest places to make secure territory, it makes sense to occupy them first, and the opening strategies commonly used for the first few thousand years of the game's existence involved taking the corners first, then the sides. Next there was usually some tactical squabbling about how much of these areas were really secure, and the centre of the board was left to last.

This is still regarded as the normal way to play the game, but various alternatives have been experimented with in the last 60 years or so. The most durable of these involve surrounding areas more loosely, and going for speed more than for solidity. Some actual examples follow.

HOW FAR APART TO PUT THE STONES

It is not necessary, at the beginning of the game, to play your stones right next to one another. A small space between them still leaves any opposing stone heavily outnumbered should it invade.

But if your stones are too far apart, there is a danger that your opponent might invade the space between, and then be able to add further stones so as to prepare attacks on both sides of your position at once. The stronger your positions are, the smaller the danger of such a counterattack, and the better your chances of actually capturing any invader. A good rough guideline is that for positions near the edge, you can afford to leave a space one line wider than the number of stones you are extending from.

So in diagram 2, where Black has a 'wall' of two stones, the extension at 1 which leaves three spaces open is about right. Add an extra stone at A, and B will become the appropriate extension. Or with A and C added to the wall, extend to D.

Diagram 3, on the next page, shows how a game might begin. Black's two-stone formation with 1 and 5 is regarded as the best way to claim corner territory when there are no opposing stones nearby.

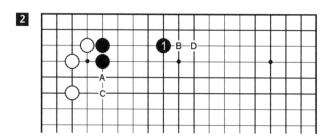

AN EXAMPLE OPENING

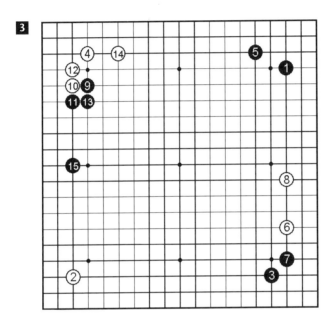

In the lower right area, Black is content to surround the corner on a slightly smaller scale, since there are white stones in the vicinity.

The extending moves at 8 and 15 are examples of our recommended strategy, leaving two empty spaces beside a single stone, and three beside a two-stone wall (the third stone at 9 is not regarded as part of this count, as it is not helping much to surround the left side).

These extending moves, at 8 and 15, are regarded as very important. Having committed yourself so far as to play a group of stones it is worth adding an extra one so that they surround some territory, and have an area in which to build eyes when the time comes to secure them.

THE THIRD AND FOURTH LINES

The strategy described on the previous page works very well at any level. You form your stones into groups each of which has enough space to make eyes and still surrounds some territory securely enough that the opponent cannot usefully invade.

An alternative approach is illustrated in diagram 4. Here the game starts with most of the stones on the fourth line, and Black quickly develops an enormous sphere of influence in the lower right area. This area is too loosely surrounded to be called territory, and White is expected to play inside it rather soon. Black is not (yet) claiming to have territory at any particular point within the area.

But Black's area is so big that White will have to invade sometime: Black's intention is to find moves which threaten to attack the invader at the same time as solidifying the remainder of the original area.

This process starts with White's move 8, which plays inside the first corner Black occupied. Instead of trying to kill this stone directly Black threatens to surround it with moves 9 and 11. White is allowed to take a small secure corner territory, but in exchange Black is able to add several stones in succession to the larger-scale project.

The sequence from 8 to 13 is typical of exchanges in the early part of the game. The players will often prefer to trade positions in a relatively peaceful way when there is still plenty of open space to claim. But as the game progresses, the Black area will still be too big to allow it all to become territory, and White will probably invade again. Next time Black may choose to attack the invading stones more vigorously, perhaps playing to prevent them from having room to make two eyes so that the white group has to escape into the centre of the board.

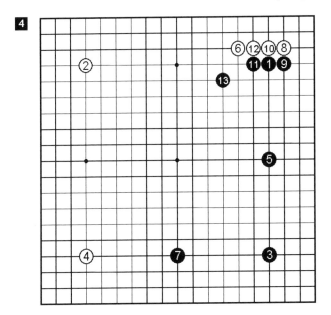

As the game continues, there may be several groups of stones on both sides which have more or less completely survived by escaping into the centre of the board. Then the whole game can come down to a struggle for survival, with both sides trying to kill the other. The middle of the board then stops being relatively unimportant and becomes the main focus of attention.

It is quite impossible to survey the whole of large-scale Go strategy in two pages, but hopefully you begin to glimpse the rich variety of different approaches available. You can choose between slow, solid play and fast and flighty; between patient trading of positions and aggressively contesting your opponent's claims; between invading immediately when it is easy and waiting until the last possible minute when it may be more efficient.

PUSHING FIGHTS

The first few moves of the game normally involve each player beginning to build positions in different areas. To start with these will often be quite loosely surrounded, but however secure the areas are there will be some sort of dividing line between them.

The closer together the two players' positions are, the more important it becomes to contest the region where the boundaries meet. When there are two lines of stones extending in contact with each other the game will often look much like the "territory game" described on page 24.

Diagram 5 shows an example. Here Black has started with three stones in this corner of the board (notice from the prickly edges of this diagram that here we are looking at the upper right corner of a full-sized board, not the 9-line board we used in previous chapters). White invades at 1, and builds a small group of stones in the corner.

The exchange of pushing moves up to black 8 is important for both sides to continue. For example if Black played elsewhere with 4 in diagram 5, White could continue as in diagram 6. This result gives White a much larger share of the right side, and leaves Black worrying about the cutting point at A.

5

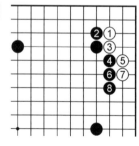

On the other hand, if White played elsewhere for move 5 in diagram 5, Black could play as in diagram 7. Now the corner will probably die, but in any case Black has walled off the right side. This means that the corner territory will be extremely small even should White manage to survive.

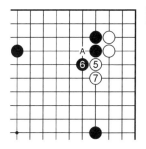

A recurring theme in these pushing fights is the value of turning moves, for example black 4 in diagram 5, white 5 in diagram 6, and black 8 and 10 in diagram 7.

These plays are particularly good at hampering your opponent's progress as well as developing your own position, and if it is possible to play such a move while giving atari to the opponent's stones, as at 10 in diagram 7, then it is even better.

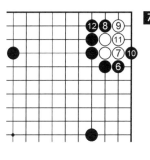

Have another look at the sequence in diagram 7, to see just how awful the result is for White. Those stones in the corner are not surrounding any territory, or threatening to surround any black stones, or separating any black positions from each other. The black stones surrounding them, on the other hand, are making good progress towards building territory on the top edge and on the right, and in addition they have almost completed the capture of the white corner.

An essential part of Go strategy is to avoid having your stones treated like these white ones, and a central part of the way in which forcing sequences work is to threaten attacks like this.

In practice, this means that when a pushing fight like the one in diagram 5 arises, both sides should continue playing in that area until their groups of stones are convincingly settled.

There is no one best way to play, and there is no substitute for trying out your ideas over the board to find which ways suit you best.

LARGE-SCALE DIVIDING LINES

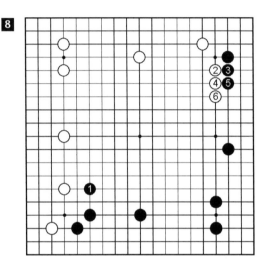

D iagram 8 shows some more examples of dividing lines. In this game both sides have concentrated on building their own area on a very large scale.

Black's play at 1 is extremely powerful. This expands the black sphere of influence at the same time as reducing the white one. It also works towards an invasion of the white position on the left.

But White 2 is also a very good move. This threatens to isolate the black stone in the upper right corner at the same time as expanding the white area at the top and preventing Black from taking the right side on a big scale. It is not very often that the opportunity arises to do so many useful things all at once. Plays like the ones in this diagram take a very high priority in the game.

CHAPTER FIVE:
INVASIONS

I n this chapter we return to the question of what secure territory looks
like. Recalling that your territory consists of the areas where you expect
to kill any stone which the opponent plays, this comes down mainly to a
question of how to invade and how to kill.

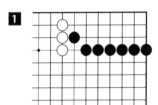

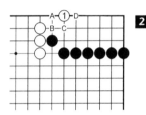

T he most common way to reduce a position dominated by your
opponent's stones is to add to your own surrounding positions,
playing stones which can connect to others for which you have already
formed eyes. In diagram 1, for example, the black area in the corner is surrounded except for the gap on the left. It would be difficult for White to
form a separate living group in the corner, but Black's area can be
substantially reduced by playing at 1 in diagram 2. White can also play 1
safely at A, B, C and, surprisingly, D. It is difficult for Black to prevent any
of these moves from creeping still further into the corner.

T he Black position in diagram 3, by
contrast, is pretty safe. You may like to
experiment a bit on a board with sequences
by which White can attempt to survive inside
this area before turning the page.

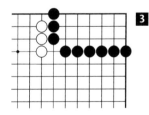

STEAL SPACE BUT LEAVE NO HOSTAGES

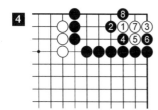

Diagram 4 shows a typical attempt by White to survive in the black corner, and also shows the recommended way to destroy the invader. Actually, an experienced player would not play any of these stones: the white ones are pointless since White is sure to die and the black ones are unnecessary since White can be killed anyway. But these moves crush the invading group completely.

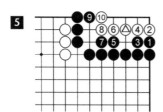

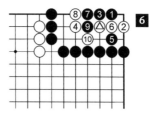

Diagrams 5 and 6 show two ways in which Black might fail to kill the invader. In diagram 5, Black plays too conservatively, concentrating only on playing stones which are absolutely safely connected. This allows White time to surround some space along the edge and make room for two eyes.

In diagram 6 Black plays too far from safety, and by aggressively trying to occupy all of the space in which White might make eyes leaves a chain of stones open to capture. When White plays at 10, the four black stones are doomed, and again White has enough space to live.

The trick of killing is to find the right balance between these extremes, and the general recommendation is to err on the side of caution. Covering your own weaknesses first leaves you free to attack anywhere.

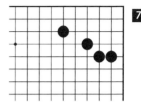

D iagram 7 shows a much less secure black area. Now the stones are farther from the corner, and there is sufficient space on the upper side for White to creep out along it. It should still be possible to kill an invasion of this corner, but it requires more precise technique than the last example.

W hite 1 in diagram 8 is a good try. Black attacks in the recommended way by patching up the weaknesses first. The blocking moves at 2 and 4 reduce White's space to a reasonable extent while concentrating mainly on making sure that the black stones are securely connected. White 5 prevents Black from capturing the stone 3 for the moment while attempting to divide the corner space into two separate eyes.

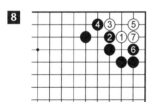

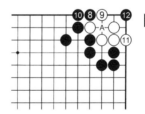

B lack 6 and 8 doggedly continue to whittle down White's space without leaving any weaknesses, and White attempts to create complications by forming a Ko shape with 9.

Black is not concerned by this attempt, however. The solid connection at 10 leaves too small a corner. Only now that there are no weaknesses left in the black surrounding wall is it time to start the progressive sacrifice manoeuvre by killing the group with 12. White A is a false eye and the corner is dead.

CHAPTER 5

A CORNER WITH ROOM TO INVADE

Now for a corner where there is room to invade. Diagram 10 shows a black position consisting of just the one stone at the star point in the upper right corner. White can invade as shown, at the 3-3 point, and can expect to form a living group of stones reasonably easily.

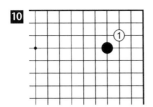

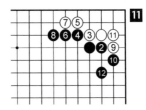

Diagram 11 shows the standard continuation. Black is not trying particularly hard to kill the corner stones, and is concentrating instead on building as secure a position as possible on the outside while White is busy looking after the corner. When Black protects a cutting point with 12 neither side has urgent things left to do in the area.

Notice that Black's approach to this position is very similar to that on the previous page where the intention was to kill the invading stones. In both cases Black concentrates first on shutting the stones into the corner without leaving White any scope for counterattack, and only having done that is it worth looking at what can be done to kill the corner.

Since Black plays pretty much the same way whether the invader is expected to die or not, there is no need to calculate exactly what is going to happen, and this can save a lot of difficult thinking. When your position is invaded, shutting the invader inside as secure a wall as you can manage and then looking to see what you have caught provides a good general purpose strategy.

The corner with one stone on the star point leaves room for an invasion to survive. Now we look at a couple of examples nearer to the borderline. Do not worry too much about the details here at first, the main thing is to get an idea of roughly how many stones you have to play in a corner to be able to claim it as territory.

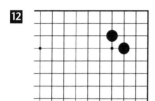
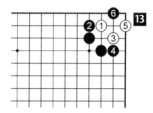

The two black stones in diagram 12, both on the third line from the edge, are sufficient to take a secure hold on the corner. If White starts to build a group inside as in diagram 13 it should die quite cleanly. White 5 there threatens to build the smallest possible living group by playing at 6, but black 6 makes quite sure there will only be one eye.

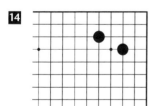
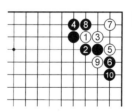

Diagram 14 shows a black formation which is one line looser. Now White has enough space to stir up some trouble, as in diagram 15 for example, and Black needs to play more precisely to suppress the invader. This should work for Black, and the result of diagram 15 is a disaster for White. The formation in diagram 14 is regarded as the best way for experienced players to claim a corner in the early part of the game.

CHAPTER 5

INVASIONS WHICH NEED A BIT OF HELP

Playing inside a corner where your opponent has the first stone is already a bit of a struggle. If there are two stones around the corner the invader needs a bit of help to be able to make enough space. Here we look at some of the forms this help might take.

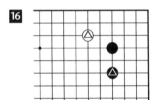

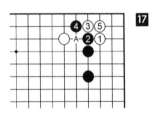

In diagram 16, Black has an extra stone supporting the corner, but White has the marked stone on the outside, and this extra white stone gives some very useful support to the invasion at the 3-3 point.

White invades at 1 in diagram 17. White can get a reasonable result either by connecting all the stones together along the top or by occupying the corner. Here we suppose that Black tries to keep the white stones separated.

The white stone on the outside now starts to do some work, since Black is kept so busy maintaining the separation that White gets time to add some extra stones in the corner. White 3 and 5 in diagram 17 already make almost enough space to live in the corner and Black still needs to prevent the cut

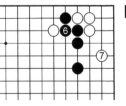

at A. Diagram 18 completes the sequence. Black seals off the outside with 6 and White uses the extra time gained to expand the corner with 7.

COUNTERATTACK

W e have seen that a corner territory surrounded by as few as two stones is already strong enough to have a good shot at killing any invading stones, but extra possibilities appear when the surrounding wall is itself surrounded on the outside.

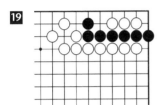

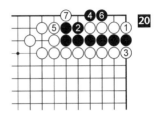

D iagram 19 shows the sort of thing to aim at. Here the three white stones in the corner are surrounded, and they have not enough room to form two eyes along the edge, but the entire surrounding black wall can come under attack.

White plays at 1 in diagram 20. At this point, White is not actually trying to make a permanently living shape, but just wants to hang on for long enough to be able to engulf and capture the surrounding wall. Black tries to capture the corner stones as fast as possible, but White is going to be faster in this situation. White 7 is atari on eight black stones, and there is no escape.

Looking at this one from a defender's point of view, the story is that you need to start taking care over your defence when what seem to be apparently solid positions start to lose their outside liberties. There is a further implication too, that even when you have a strong position and are confident that you can take away the eyes from any invader, it is still worth connecting to your other positions along the sides and in the centre of the board.

SEKI –
NEITHER SIDE CAN KILL

The kind of life and death fight we saw in diagram 19 often ends up with one side or other being captured, but there is a third possibility; a stand-off in which neither side can capture the other.

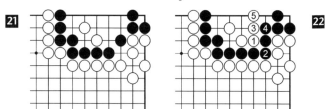

Diagram 21 shows a black group which has reached the stage we described as worrying – it is surrounded on the outside and White can start attacking by filling in its inside liberties. Diagram 22 shows the beginning of this process. White gets off to a good start by playing forcing moves at 1 and 3, and then makes sure of having at least one eye with 5.

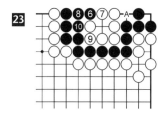

Black continues to try to capture the white group up to 10, but then there is a stand-off. Neither side can play at A since the opponent would reply by capturing their entire group. Neither side scores any territory and the stones stay as they are at the end of the game. White has succeeded in reducing the black territory, but both sides have failed to kill.

This sort of stand-off is called Seki in Japanese. Its key feature is that neither side can afford to fill the last liberty separating the groups.

PROBLEMS

$\mathcal{E}$ach of these positions shows a black area which White has started to invade. The problem in each case is, How well is White doing? Is the invasion already safe? Can it survive with one extra move from White, but be killed if Black plays first, or is it already hopeless without Black requiring another play?

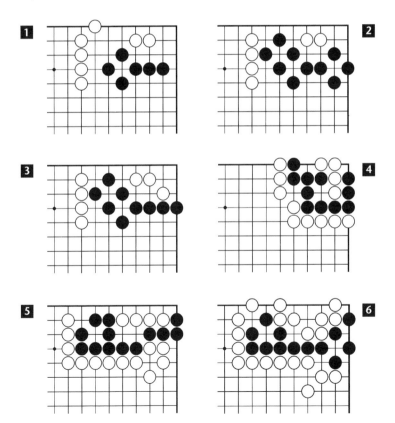

SOLUTIONS TO PROBLEMS

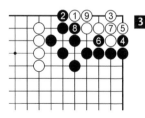

1

White is already safe. There is no way for Black to separate the two stones in the corner from the ones on the outside. The sequence shown is no good, since White can capture Black's stone at 3.

2

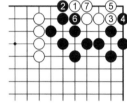

White is dead without Black requiring a further play. White can threaten to connect along the edge with 1, but the most that can be hoped for is one eye, and the surrounding black stones have plenty of eyes and plenty of liberties, so there is no counterattack.

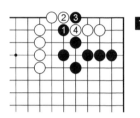

3

Here White can live as shown. The important play is 3 which divides the corner space into two separate eyes. If Black plays first, the corner can be killed in several ways of which the sequence 4, 5, 3 is safest.

This is an example of Seki. Neither side can capture the other. Black might try filling a liberty with 1 here but White can take the last outside liberty in reply, and now neither side can play at A or B without being captured when the opponent takes the other spot.

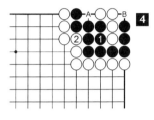

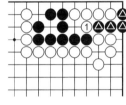

White can capture the entire black formation by cutting at 1 here. This captures the marked stones, after which the remaining black group has only one eye. If Black plays first, connecting at 1 is necessary. Then there will be time for Black to capture the four stones.

White is alive without further play. The invading stones can either connect to the outside at A or make eyes at B, and Black cannot prevent both of these things from happening. And the black stones are all dead for a similar reason. White can steal one eye or the other by playing at C or D.

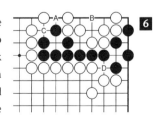

CHAPTER SIX:
ATTACK AND DEFENCE

So far, we have dealt mainly with situations in which the two players' stones are quite close together, and the main threats to stones are threats of immediate capture. An understanding of the possibilities in these situations is essential if you are to play effectively. As your experience of local situations expands, it becomes possible to guess fairly accurately what the result of a tactical skirmish would be, and to avoid those with unfavourable results.

This introduces a new level of pressure to put on your opponent. Rather than actually threatening immediate capture, you can use broader threats to make those threats effectively. This may all sound a bit abstract and remote, but for the purposes of this chapter we will concentrate on one particular fact and its effect on the game: it is bad to have your stones surrounded, even if they are going to live.

Diagram 1 shows the sort of result we are interested in. The marked black stone surrounds the two white ones on the upper side rather loosely. White needs to find some space to build eyes, and this can be done fairly easily. In diagram 2, White pushes out against all the gaps in the black wall to surround a space which looks just about big enough.

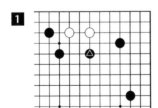

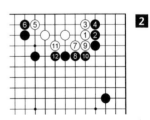

But diagram 2 is a terrible result for White, whether or not those stones are alive. Black started in diagram 1 with a very feeble looking string of four stones around the white group, and now has a secure wall of ten stones without having to spend any extra moves building it.

t is important to realise that the result in diagram 2 is bad for White even if the stones are alive. When this sort of thing occurs in a game the result can be much worse. In addition to the splendid wall which Black has been allowed to build, the white stones may well have an accident later on and fail to make two eyes securely. Once your stones have been completely surrounded, any small miscalculation can result in them being captured cleanly. An escape route to the centre as extra insurance means that you can afford to be less precise in your calculation.

The usual way to avoid being surrounded, if possible, is to extend your group along the sides of the board. This is usually on the third or fourth lines from the edge, making some territory at the same time. But when this is not possible, the centre of the board becomes important.

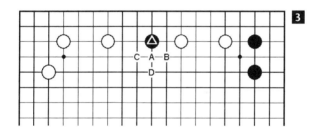

D iagram 3 shows a typical position from the early stage of a game. Black has a stone isolated on the upper side of the board, and has no room to establish a base of territory along the side. Black's strategy will be to form a group of stones running out into the centre of the board, and any of the points A, B, C or D would help achieve this aim.

Of these points, A is a bit too slow and solid, B and C are reasonable, but D is the standard point to play. This "one-point jump" is much the most common move to see in such situations, striking a reasonable balance between being securely connected and escaping quickly.

WHAT IF?

There is an immediate practical problem with the 'one-point jump' we are recommending. What if the opponent tries to separate the stones, as in diagram 4?

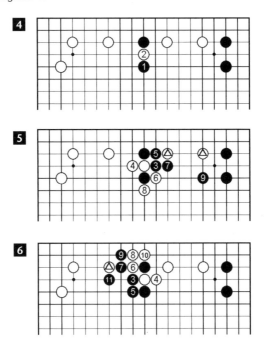

Black has several ways to respond to this attack, playing atari on one side of the white stone and then choosing which of the cutting points to connect. The result usually involves a small sacrifice and a large gain. Diagrams 5 and 6 both produce satisfactory attacks on the stones marked. Black has a choice as to which direction to start these manoeuvres, and usually at least one of the choices is effective.

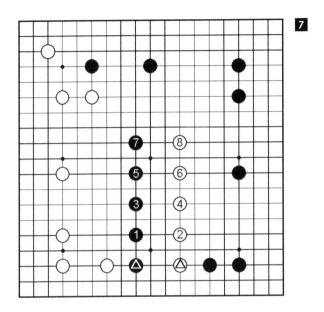

Once a group of stones has started making one-point jumps into the middle of the board, it is often a good idea to continue with them. Diagram 7 shows an example where both sides start with an isolated stone near the lower edge. Neither side wishes to be surrounded, and both are interested in reducing the other's sphere of influence.

It is not so much a question of defending the stones against immediate capture as of preventing the question of capture from being raised. Once a group of stones is surrounded they become a worry, and cramp the player's options for doing anything else in that area of the board. Suppose, for example, that White decides to strengthen the left side territory instead of playing at 8 in this diagram. Try to picture the result before you turn the page.

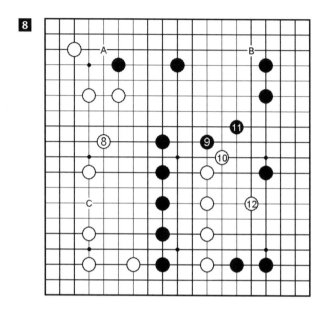

White strengthens the left side by playing move 8 as shown here. Now Black has the opportunity to turn on the stones on the right. The 'capping play' at 9 in combination with black 11 is particularly effective in blocking White's access to the upper side. Now White starts worrying about where exactly this group of stones is going to find two eyes. Move 12 starts creating a little space in the centre, but White still has to worry, and meanwhile Black has made giant strides towards surrounding the top of the board on a huge scale. Next Black can choose between expanding the upper area with A, solidifying it with B, or perhaps trying an invasion of the white side at the remaining gap of C.

Notice here that White has added one stone to the left side and spent a move doing it. Black however has added two stones to the upper side and, since White answered them, spent no moves.

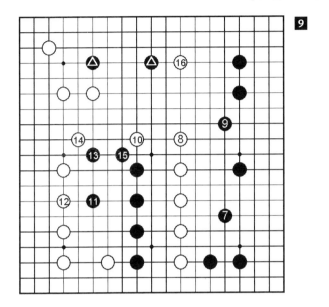

Just for the sake of completion, let us see what happens if Black makes the same mistake. Here, time is taken to surround some territory with 7 and 9 instead of continuing to run with the stones in the centre.

Now it is White who gets to play the key 'capping' play at 10, and Black who has to surround a small territory in the centre in order to be able to make two eyes.

This time White gets to play two stones strengthening the left side, and the upper area is a great deal farther from becoming black territory than before. White can invade somewhere around 16, and may even succeed in separating and attacking the two marked stones in the upper left area. Black is reduced to defending all over the board.

Compare these two diagrams and see how the notions of attack, defence and efficiency interact across the board.

WHY RUNNING AWAY WORKS

Many players' first impulse when they learn the capturing game is to start filling in the liberties of the opponent's stones as quickly as possible. This produces a pattern rather like Diagram 10, however. Black is running away with a group of stones while White attempts to chase after it from both sides at once.

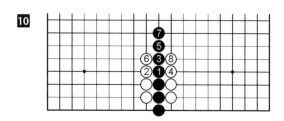

This does not work. The black stones run twice as fast because Black is running with only one group of stones compared to White's two. This basic fact describes the main attraction of running into the centre with your weak stones – the side running away is twice as fast as the pursuer.

There are additional attractions for Black in running towards the centre, and these apply whether the group is itself weak or not:

♦ The stones act as support for Black's next invasion, giving something to connect up to for safety.

♦ They prepare to attack adjacent groups on both sides. Black does not suffer from the usual two-to-one disadvantage in these attacks since there is no need to launch an attack on one side until after White has chosen to defend on the other.

♦ It may be possible to make some territory in the centre of the board later. This is a relatively minor consideration in most cases, since it is notoriously difficult to complete a territory in the centre. There are too many sides from which to reduce it without having to make a separate invasion.

Diagram 10 does not work for White. Once a group of stones has escaped into the centre of the board there is no future in attacking it directly. White does much better by playing something like Diagram 11:

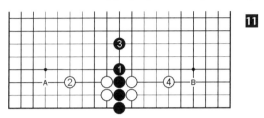

Here White takes advantage of the time that Black uses in running away to settle the stones on each side. Black follows the recommended practice of defending as a first priority with 3, and after white 4 has a choice of which side to attack. In this rather artificial example, the two points A and B are exactly equivalent. More typically there would be some reason to prefer one side.

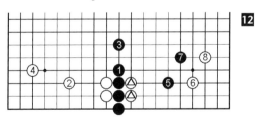

But actually, if these were the only stones on the board, White would be better advised not trying to hang on to everything after black 3. It is easier, and usually more profitable, not to fight near your opponent's strong stones. White can sketch out a large corner with 4 in diagram 12, and if Black is determined to attack the two marked stones – with 5 for example – White does well by taking the other corner. Black may make 20 points in the area around the two captured stones, but White should do better, making 15 points on each side.

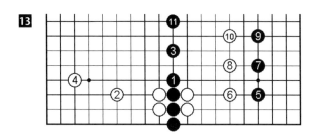

C ontinuing with the example from the previous page, if Black cannot get a good result by capturing the two loose stones left behind by white 4 here, how about letting them escape?

Black 5 in diagram 13 is nearer to the truth. This aims to surround the two white stones on a large enough scale to make it worthwhile. Now White has just about enough room to build a living group of stones, but it is a little cramped, and needs to run out into the centre to avoid being enclosed tightly.

While White is building this group of stones, Black has time to make some territory around the lower right corner. This result looks reasonable for both sides. Each has found time to surround some territory in a corner, each has a slightly weak group of stones running out into the centre, and the game is in balance.

The process we have been following through the last two pages is typical of the sort of continuous refinement involved in selecting a good point to play on. By imagining the possible continuations and steering between overconcentration and weakness, attack and defence, territory now and security for later – and a host of other conflicting objectives – your game moves organically towards perfect balance.

CHAPTER SEVEN: TACTICAL TRICKS

The game of Go is full of patterns which special tricks are associated with. This chapter concentrates on a small family of them, those involving the use of sacrifice stones to reduce your opponent's liberties. Chances to use these are common in games, and the result is often devastating.

Take a look at diagram 1. The three black stones on the right are in trouble. They have only two liberties, and no room to escape. Black will have to capture some of the surrounding stones very quickly if anything is to be done.

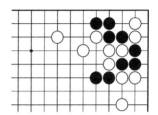

The trick here is to sacrifice a stone at 1 in diagram 2. White can capture this stone immediately with 2, but now Black has 3, which is atari on four white stones at the same time as it reaches around the entire white group. When White connects at 1 with move 4, the whole group only has the two liberties at A and B. Black can then continue as in diagram 3, capturing as many stones as White is obstinate enough to add. White would have done better to abandon the whole area after 1 in diagram 2.

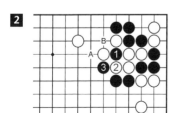

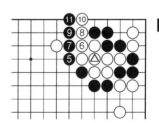

Play through this sequence on the board a few times, and see how much you can discover about the way the black stones are working.

SNAPBACK

The key to the sequence on the previous page lies in the stones shown below in diagram 4. The two black stones marked with triangles ensure that the point A can only be a false eye for White, and the chance of sacrificing a black stone at A to reduce White's liberties is always a threat in this shape. Here it is good for Black to play at A immediately.

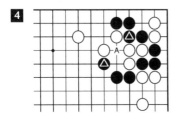

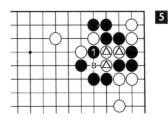

Black 1 in diagram 5 creates a shape known as the "snapback". Black 1 is atari on four white stones, but if White captures black 1 by replying at B, Black can play a second stone at 1 and capture four white stones. The stone at B fills in White's own liberty.

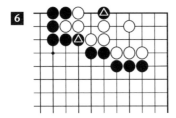

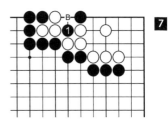

Diagram 6 shows another variant of the snapback. Black's two marked stones again create a false eye, and when Black offers the sacrifice stone at 1 in diagram 7 the capture at B fills in White's own liberty.

THROW-IN

Moving the position still closer to the edge of the board, we arrive at diagram 8, where Black can capture four stones in snapback by playing at 1 in diagram 9. White's capture at B fails in the same way as before.

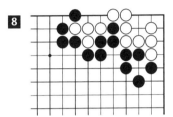

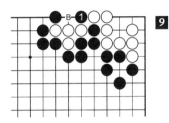

The kind of shape which White has here, with stones connecting together along the first and second lines on the edge of the board, is extremely common. Such positions are always vulnerable to the snapback, or to a similar type of liberty shortage caused by the "Throw-in".

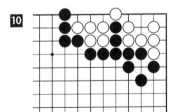

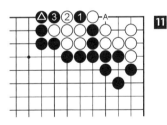

Diagram 10 shows a white group vulnerable to capture, and diagram 11 shows how to capture part of it. Black 1 is the throw-in, which reduces White's liberties without allowing a chance to connect any of the weak points. Black 3 puts six white stones into atari, and it is too late for White to rescue them, since Black is sure to have a chance to capture either at 1 or at A. Notice that the marked black stone is important for this process to work.

FALSE EYES COST LIBERTIES

The key to the sort of liberty shortage problem which we have just seen is that the vulnerable group has a number of false eyes along the edge. In order for White to connect all the stones together in time, it is necessary to play white stones on all the false eyes. The point of the throw-in trick is to keep White busy while Black fills in some of the outside liberties.

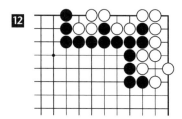

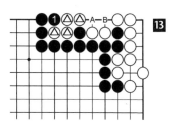

Sometimes it is not necessary to play any sacrifice stones. Diagram 12 shows an example in which White has two false eyes next to each other on the edge. Here Black needs only to play atari at 1 in diagram 13 to leave the four marked stones helpless. White would need to connect at both A and B to make them safe.

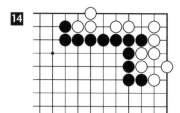

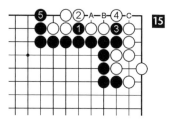

Diagram 14 shows how such a position might arise. The white stones cannot be separated, but by pushing in at 1 and 3 in diagram 15, Black creates three false eyes, at A, B, and C. This leaves enough time to play the key approaching move at 5. White has no defence.

STARTING A KO FIGHT

The approach stone at 5 in diagram 15 is important to the process of capturing a group of stones along the edge. Often there is not enough time to play this stone, but a black stone one line farther away can be enough to cause trouble.

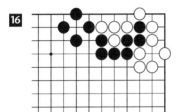

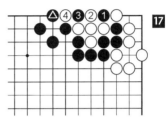

The basic shape is shown in diagram 16. The black stone on the first line is one space too far away to capture the four stones cleanly with a throw in, but the sequence in diagram 17 gives a chance of capture. After the black atari at 3, White can capture at 4, but this is the ko shape. If Black can find a threatening move elsewhere on the board and force White to reply then it becomes legal to recapture at 3. White will then look for a threat, and so on. Black can expect either to capture some stones in this area or to get two moves in a row somewhere else.

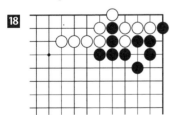

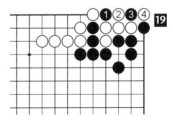

Diagram 18 shows a similar structure. Black starts a ko fight with 1 and 3 in diagram 19. Possibilities to start ko fights like this often occur in games, once you get to know where to look for them.

PROBLEMS

In each of these positions, Black is to play and find a way to capture some white stones. All of them involve liberty shortages of some sort. The last two are rather more difficult than the others.

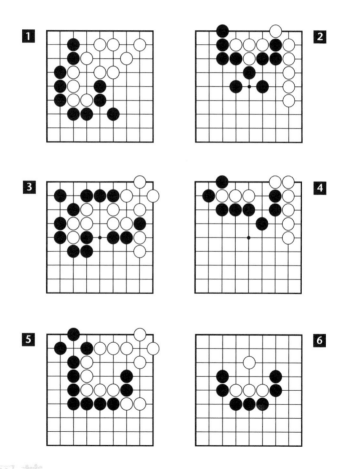

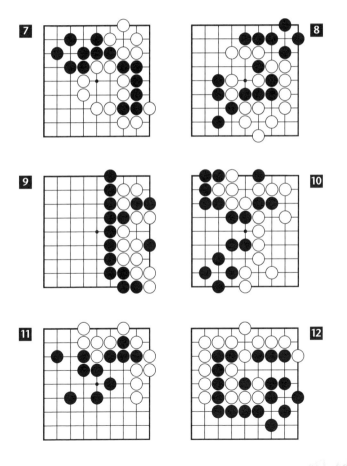

CHAPTER 7

SOLUTIONS TO PROBLEMS 1–6

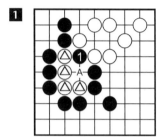

Black 1 catches the four marked white stones in a snapback. Their only remaining liberty is at A, but in order to capture the black sacrifice stone White has to play at A. The five white stones then only have one liberty, at 1, and Black plays back there again to capture them.

Black reduces the liberties of the stones on the upper side using the throw-in sacrifice at 1. This gives Black time to play atari at 3 before White has protected either of the weak points, at 1 and A. White could try playing 2 at A, but then black 3 creates a snapback, and the stones are still captured.

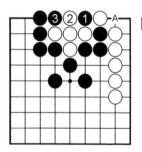

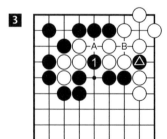

The marked black stone is dead, but it still has some use. Black 1 is atari on the four stones to the left, but if they connect up at A, Black can capture eight stones by playing B. The other atari (at A) is no use to Black. White could then connect safely, having a second central liberty.

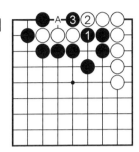

Black pushes into the top side with 1, creating the right shape for the snapback at 3. White can capture a stone by playing at A, but a second black play at 3 captures four stones. Starting with black 1 at 2 would not work: White would play 1 – getting an extra liberty below 1 – and survive.

Black must cut at 1 immediately. Anything else would allow White to connect there. Now that White is helpless, the atari at 2 allows Black to create the snapback shape as shown, and white trying 3 instead allows black to play at 2.

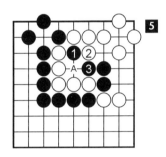

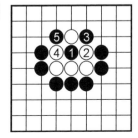

This position comes from a famous shape known as the "Crane's Nest". The three white "eggs" have tried to escape by jumping into the centre, but Black can sacrifice a stone at 1 and reduce the white group to one liberty surprisingly fast.

SOLUTIONS TO PROBLEMS 7–12

7

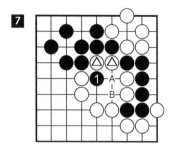

Black can make a capture by playing at 1, A, or B, but only black 1 makes sure of capturing the two marked stones, and it is only by capturing these stones that Black can survive. If White rescues the marked stones and loses the two by A and B, Black will only have one eye and the whole group will die.

This is another case in which you have to play the right atari in order to be sure of capturing the cutting stones. Black A would capture a stone for the moment, but the whole six-stone group Black built by doing so would only have one eye, and would die when White rescued the key stones by playing at 1.

8

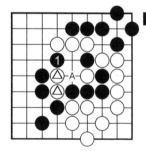

9

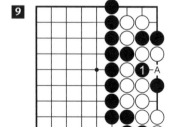

Black 1 makes the snapback shape, and White cannot avoid capture with A. The two white stones above can escape by capturing two black ones, but black 1 is also atari on the eight stones in the lower corner, and they have no escape.

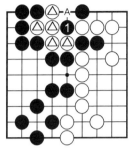

This example of snapback allows Black to rescue three very dead stones and capture five healthy-looking white ones. The shape is essentially the same as before, but the edge of the board is doing a lot of the work for Black.

White has two outside liberties (at 3 and 7), but the shape in the corner takes a long time to tidy up. Provided that Black creates a false eye by sacrificing a stone at 1, and plays one of the points 4 and 5, there will be time to catch White in a shortage of liberties.

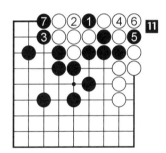

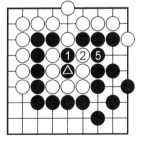

White must be prevented from making an eye at the triangled point, so Black sacrifices a second stone at 1, and then plays 3 at 1 again. White 4, at the marked point, captures a stone but only makes a false eye. Now Black can fill a liberty at 5 and White cannot escape from atari.

CHAPTER EIGHT: AN ADVANCED GAME

THE FINAL OF THE 1980 EUROPEAN CHAMPIONSHIP

The annual European Championships are a two-week festival of Go, with competitions for all levels of players. The premier tournament in 1980 was a round robin event between the top 20 or so players. Each entrant played nine games, at the rate of one game per day. In the event of a tie, a playoff game would determine the overall winner.

The competition had been dominated throughout the 1960s and 1970s by German and Austrian players, and Jürgen Mattern, born in Berlin in 1944, was particularly successful towards the end of that period. He was the reigning Champion, and was clearly the man to beat.

I had attended my first European Congress in 1975, and started playing in the championship group in 1977. My first three attempts had yielded fourth, third and fifth places, confirming a position near the top but still leaving plenty to prove.

The tournament was held on the Adriatic island of Mali Lošinj, then in Yugoslavia. It was an ideal place for a seaside holiday, but many players found it too hot to maintain concentration through the six-hour games. Physical stamina is important for success in such events.

After two weeks, there were two players with eight wins from nine, so a tenth game would determine the European Champion. This chapter follows that game, with commentary describing the flow of the match.

Mattern was a very steady player who preferred to take few risks on, waiting for a chance to reverse any setback later on by accumulating small advantages. At the time, I was playing a much riskier strategy, experimenting freely in the early stages and challenging my opponents to join in decisive fights at every stage of the game. I had the black stones, and started off with the unconventional combination shown in Figure 1.

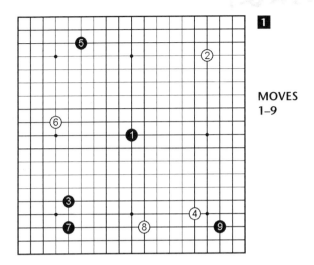

1

**MOVES
1–9**

Playing the first move of the game in the centre has been tried occasionally over the years at all levels. This point is not much use for surrounding territory directly, and if the game develops into a passive one in which both sides surround their own territory this stone can become almost worthless. Black's plan here is to force the game into a pattern in which there are weak groups chasing each other around the board, and to pick up territory here and there as the fighting progresses.

Black continues by surrounding the two corners on the left with very remote stones. Normally Black's stones 3 and 5 would be too far away to claim the corners securely enough, but White is being offered a choice of letting the corners become secure on a larger-than-usual scale, or invading them and creating what may become weak groups.

White's moves 2 and 4 are also rather far from their corners. Black is being offered a chance to make small invading groups in these areas, which would involve abandoning the centrally-oriented strategy implied by the first move. Black goes for the first real invasion of the game with 9.

The sequence from 10 to 13 leaves the lower right area more or less settled for now. Black has a greater share of the corner and can expand along the right, while White has a territory on the lower side which is secure enough for the moment.

White adds a stone at 14 in the upper right, and then Black has the task of trying to develop the left side. Black 15 is too far away from the lower corner to make secure territory yet, but it also threatens to take away any eye-making space from the marked white stone. Black is hoping to maintain an attack on this stone for long enough to be able to add a series of reinforcing stones to the lower left area, and surround it as territory on a big scale.

White counters at 16. He is defending the triangled stone rather indirectly, and hoping to claim a share of the upper corner while doing so. In response Black decides to abandon the triangled stone on the upper side for the moment so as to pursue the attack on the left. After 21 White is doing well in the upper corner, but the marked white stone on the left side is awkwardly placed. It is being surrounded on too large a scale to be simply abandoned, and White wants to keep the option of invading the lower left corner available for later.

The three black stones at 17, 19 and 21 do not form a particularly powerful attack on the white stones above or below. The problem for White is that they do threaten to do damage in both directions, and White has only one move at a time to answer both threats. Running out into the centre of the board with one-point jumps like this is often a very powerful way to play. If it also leads a weak group of your own stones into the centre and out of danger it is even better.

White is not able to rescue the marked stone on the left in such a clear fashion, since there is a black stone waiting in the centre of the board to get in the way. White will have to tread very delicately on the left to prevent a large black territory from appearing somewhere.

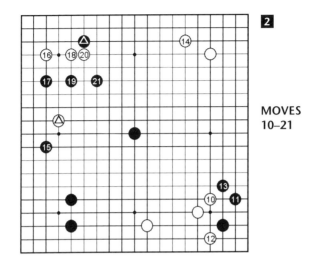

2

**MOVES
10–21**

Reviewing the progress of the game so far: White has built three fairly solid positions, in the two upper corners and on the lower side, while Black has a small position in the lower right and is also staking out a large sphere of influence on the left. Black would require another two or three plays on the left side to convert all of this area into solid territory, but that would make more than enough to win, whatever White did elsewhere. The white positions simply do not have as much space for expansion on a large scale. White is going to have to establish at least one signifcant living group of stones in this left area, and immediately is going to be the best time to start.

In terms of large-scale strategy and control of the game, Black's initial plan of producing a large-scale game with weak groups struggling for life in the centre is doing quite well. The skill with which these groups are managed will probably be decisive.

W hite decides to try to establish a living group on the left and play an extra stone expanding the upper side as well. The method is to play forcing moves at 22 and 24 before adding 26 to the top.

White 26 is an interesting idea. This stone is not particularly good at capturing the loose black stone at the top – indeed, that stone gets rescued rather soon – but White is aware that his stones on the left are in some danger and part of his plan to keep them healthy is to try to develop a counterattack on the black group in the upper left (including 23, 25).

The expected Black attack starts with 27. Now Black is not trying to capture these white stones, but rather to keep them as busy as possible. This will help find time to secure the large lower left corner as well as keeping the black group at the top connected out into the centre.

Black 35 is another stone which does several jobs at once. The most urgent aim is to keep the black stones connected and 35 helps black 29 to connect in two directions at once. But 35 is also aiming to support a future invasion of the white area along the upper side. It is trying to do all these things in such a way that the white stones on the left are forced to make exchanges like 38 – 39 in order to escape.

By the end of this section the white stones on the left have almost finished connecting out to safety. White's play in the lower right area proves very useful here. His earlier choice of a secure position facing the centre means that the weak stones on the left now have somewhere safe to run.

There remains an extremely difficult question, of whether that large area in the lower left is really secure black territory or not. Answering this one precisely is too difficult for players at this level, and it comes down to experience and judgment. This corner is about the right size to make the question very difficult.

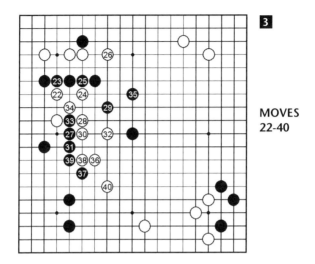

3

**MOVES
22-40**

There are some players who would spend a lot of time trying to work out the possible variations following a white invasion of the corner. It is usually easier to count the rest of the board though, and work out whether it is necessary to invade, or indeed whether the area is big enough that Black can afford to spend an extra stone making sure of it.

In this position, the whole Black corner is roughly five lines by eight, making 40 points. White has territory in three areas – the lower side and the top two corners – and can outscore Black's big corner by getting 15 points in each of these areas. The Black position in the lower right is quite small, perhaps no bigger than the 5½ points White is given as compensation for playing second. For the moment Black cannot afford to spend an extra move if White's reply would then complete the whole upper side as territory.

lack's next task was to break up the upper side of the board into small areas, so that White had no chance to win the game outright by surrounding it all. The moves to 49 leave each side with a small group of stones fairly well endowed with space for making eyes. After 49, the big black corner is looking rather too big to allow.

So White plunged in. The next few moves enabled White to plan the rest of the game. Both players were operating largely by guesswork in this sequence, but up to 61 it looked as if Black has managed to hang on to a small part of the corner while White had a good chance to squeeze out through the gap at 65.

White 62 threatens to capture one stone, and to expand along the left side by playing at 63. Black 63 ignored the threat, however. Capturing one stone only makes one eye.

**MOVES
41–68**

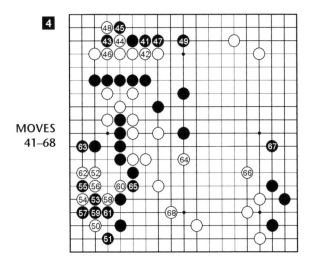

So far, the invading stones White has played have all been inside the area which Black was claiming as territory anyway. If the invasion proceeds any further, White will be totally committed to its success. A direct continuation might follow as per the example diagram A shown here. White 1 in this diagram replaces white 64 in the game.

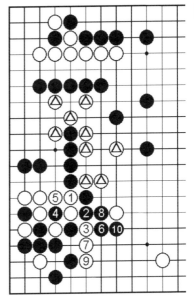

White has the more difficult position in this diagram. The black stones are likely to escape, and the marked white stones may come under attack again if they do. Rather than commit himself to doing anything like this, White chose instead to reinforce the weak stones in the centre with 64. Now the example diagram, or something like it, would be much more dangerous for Black, and completing the capture of the white group on the left with 65 is more or less forced.

In effect, the white invasion has ended up by exchanging one extra move in the centre (64) for a reinforcement of the corner. White has lost some points by exchanging 62 for 63 – which expands Black's position on the left side a little – and is now sure that there is no chance to live in the corner. White is behind in the game, but it is not over yet, and he sets to work building some territory on the lower side making use of the stone at 64. There is a gap between the stones at 64 and 66, and Black's next problem is how far to try to reach into it.

MOVES
69–90

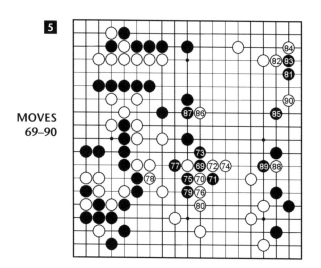

B lack 69 and 71 reach into the white area, offering a sacrifice in one direction in order to encroach in another. Up to white 80, the borders in this area are clarified, with each side capturing one stone. White 78 is necessary to prevent Black from playing there and cutting off the white stones on the left. This white group connecting across the left side continues to be a liability here, and the odd stone which Black captures at 77 is typical of the small gains to be made from having an eyeless chain of stones to threaten.

The next problem is the right side. Black's approach is to scatter stones all along the side, expecting that White will break through somewhere, and planning to solidify whichever part of the area White does not invade. Black is keeping control of the game here by pretending to claim too much in each area, and then settling for half as White struggles to find extra territory.

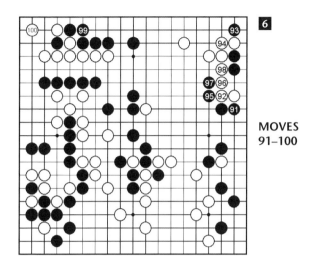

**MOVES
91–100**

B lack 91 allows the two stones above to be captured, but they have served their purpose. This involved keeping White busy while Black secured a decent proportion of the right side.

The exchange of 93 for 94 has very little effect, but depending on what happens later on the upper side the stone at 93 might possibly be useful to Black. This sort of incidental exchange is often used by experienced players to create small inefficiencies in their opponent's structures.

The main areas of territory are now spoken for, and it remains only to argue about the exact positions of the boundaries. Black 99 takes top priority here, because the black stones on the upper side and the white ones in the corner are both near to the minimum size required to be sure of making two eyes. White responds by securing the corner with 100.

I n this phase, Black continues to add stones on the right, expanding the territory there by a few points, but also beginning to surround a large swathe of the area in the centre of the board. It is normally very difficult to make much territory in the centre, because there are too many directions from which to invade. In this case Black closes one route with 107, and then White is able to come in from the other side with 108. But although there is not much actual territory in the centre, White now has an extra liability, having to make sure that 108 is able to connect to his other stones. This enables Black to steal some extra points along the top edge with 120.

The game had proceeded quite quickly, considering the time limits of three hours' thinking time each, and the lunch break did not occur until it was White's turn to play 121. The normal practice in competitions is for the player whose turn it is at lunch time to write down the next move and seal it in an envelope which the referee keeps. This way neither side can use the lunch break to prepare their next play.

White could have captured one stone by playing 120 at 121, but this would have allowed Black to separate white 108 from the upper side, using the sacrifice of 119 to get an extra stone in the centre. This would make as much territory in the centre as White had gained on the side. But when black 121 adds some extra space to the group on the upper side there is very little chance left for White to catch up.

There are several areas in which the boundaries of the territories are yet to be firmly decided. The normal course of play during the endgame stage is for the action to dot around the board, with each side trying to find the points which make the biggest difference to the territories. The main trick here is to avoid answering your opponent's moves as much as possible, so that you answer a big move in one area with an equally big move elsewhere.

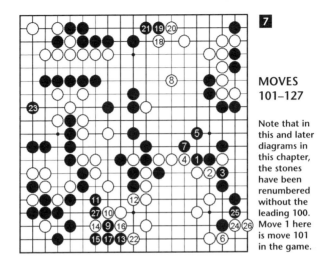

7

MOVES 101–127

Note that in this and later diagrams in this chapter, the stones have been renumbered without the leading 100. Move 1 here is move 101 in the game.

O f the big points played in this diagram, black 121 comes first because it makes sure of the life of a group of stones. White 122 is very large as well, because White would have been obliged to answer a black move in that area. Black 123 is worth some extra points because it connects the black stones along the left edge. There was a danger that White could have played in this area and later gained some points by threatening to rescue the dead stones in the lower left. Then White 124 takes a few points in the corner, but Black could also have taken a few points in the corner so the difference is bigger than with 127, which adds to the black territory in an area where White could not make any.

By the end of this figure the large points have been played, and both sides know that the game is essentially over. White is behind, and can only win if Black makes a mistake somewhere.

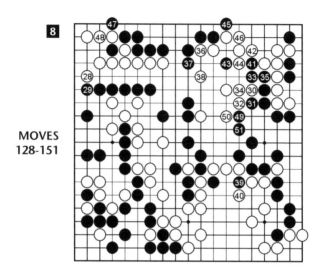

**MOVES
128-151**

The action returns to the centre area now, since all of the big points around the edge have been played. What is really going on here though is that White is trying to find a way to capture the black group on the top edge. Both sides know perfectly well that this group is big enough to be safe if Black plays correctly, but it is the last area with scope for any complications.

White's choice of 136 as a way to surround a few points in the centre is part of this process. It creates a cutting point in the black shape. Black refuses to correct this defect directly, and leaves some scope for complications with 137.

Black 143 becomes a sacrifice stone, but it allows Black to gain points with 145. For White, playing at 146 is necessary to prevent Black from cutting with atari.

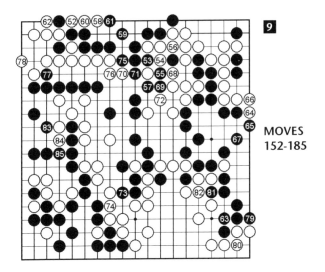

9

MOVES 152–185

White 152 crept closer to springing the white trap, but Black had calculated the possibilities carefully, and indulged in a little brinkmanship by capturing an extra stone in the centre with 153–157. See if you can work out what would happen if White had played 158 at 159, trying to cut off and capture some stones to one side or the other.

Reducing the territory with 158–162 was the best White could manage, and the rest of this diagram shows the remaining details being sorted out. Black 185 was the last move of the game. White then resigned. There was nothing interesting left to try, and he was losing by more than ten points even taking account of the 5½ point bonus for playing second at the start.

Black kept control of this game by threatening in each area to take far too much. This kept White busy, struggling to retain anywhere near an equal share. The successful capture in the lower left proved decisive.

The domination of the European Championship by German-speaking central Europe effectively ended with this game. The winners through the rest of the 1980s came from the Netherlands, Poland, Hungary and Britain, with the Dutch claim to be top Go nation in Europe probably the strongest. The European Championship was increasingly affected by the inclusion of visiting Oriental players, and Japan and Korea also feature in the winners' list.

In the last few years there has been a surge of activity in Romania. A tournament in December 1997 to select the European representative for the World Championship in 1998 from a field of 16 players saw the three Romanians winning all their games against the other nations present.

Each time the centre of gravity of European Go shifts from one country to another, the level of the top players comes closer to that of the older Go-playing nations in the Orient. There is still a considerable gap, though. Both of the players in the game described in this chapter learned most of their Go in Europe, but the process of learning involved the study of a lot of games and books from the far East. More recently, there have been opportunities for long periods of study in the East – especially in Japan – for some of the younger European players, and the rising generation of European-born players already includes two with professional qualifications in Japan.

An important factor in the improvement of European Go has been the European resident players of Eastern origin. There are always a few keen amateur players among the members of the Japanese and Korean business community, and these are welcome at Go tournaments, which are becoming progressively more international. The European Champion from 1993 to 1996 was Ms Guo Juan, a former professional in mainland China and now a Dutch citizen.

Sadly, the two players who had dominated European Go through the 1970s, Jürgen Mattern and the Austrian Manfred Wimmer, died within a few months of each other in 1985. They were both in their early fifties.

CHAPTER NINE:
CHALLENGE PROBLEMS

As you become familiar with the game of Go, there are a wide range of moves which will become obvious as good things to do. A lot more will seem fairly natural when you think about them a bit. Most of this book is devoted to introducing you to ideas of this type. They describe the basic vocabulary of the game, but they do not account for all of its colour and fascination.

There are also a range of tricks which will always feel special however much time you spend on the game. Some of these seem quite incredible the first time you meet them, and this chapter is an introduction to a few of those which cause the warmest glow of satisfaction when they actually occur in your games.

The problems here are all quite localized on the board, so that there are a relatively small number of possibilities and most of them can be solved by systematically considering all the various possible moves. But you will need to be careful that you do not abandon apparently useless lines too early in the sequence, for some are deceptive. Even if some of your stones are captured, there may be useful options in playing back into the space from which they came.

The solutions are not given in this book, but there are some hints on the next four pages. Do not expect to solve all the problems in this section at a first reading. Laying out the positions on a board and spending some time experimenting with them can be a great help, and just letting the possibilities drift around your brain for a few days can also be a way to seek inspiration.

To kep things tidy, the problems are all set on the small (9x9) board, and Black is to play. The first six problems involve killing secure-looking white stones, and the second six are centred around rescuing hopeless-looking black ones.

BLACK TO PLAY AND KILL

The six problems on this page all contain an opportunity for Black to kill something, either an entire white group or an important part of one.

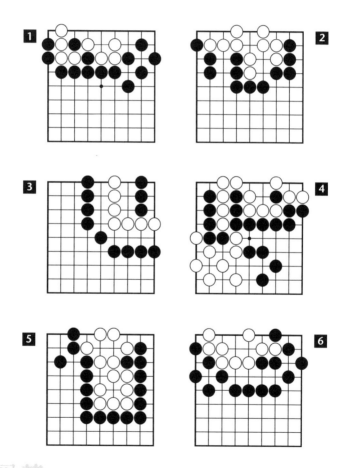

BLACK TO PLAY AND LIVE

In each of these six problems black is in immediate danger of having a group of stones killed. Only the black group at the bottom of problem 11 is safe. Your task is to rescue the stones.

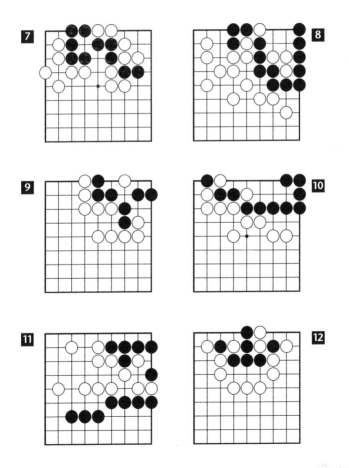

HINTS FOR PROBLEMS 1–6

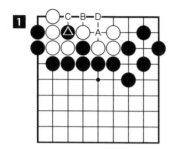

White is going to get an eye by capturing the marked stone. The other one might be at A or B. You can stop B from making a separate eye at any time by playing C with atari. Since this can be done at any time, it is best left until late.

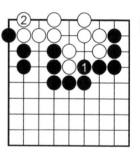

Black 1 reduces the right side to one eye, but then White 2 makes a second. Trying Black 2 would get a reply at 1, making two eyes on the right. You need to reduce the right side to one eye in a way which threatens to play a second move reducing it to none.

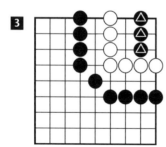

White has plenty of time to capture the marked stones, so they have to keep themselves in a shape worth only one eye when captured. White would also be happy to have both sides survive in a seki. Black has to prevent seki while keeping to a one eyed shape.

4

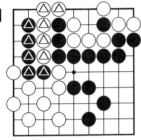

The five marked black stones are in trouble. They have no room to make two eyes in the corner, and no chance of killing the lower left white group. Their only hope lies in capturing the five marked white stones. Try everything. One possibility works!

White has a definite eye in the centre, so Black had better prevent one at the top. There are several choices here, depending on whether Black is trying to prevent an eye at A or one at B. The throw-in at A is no good at present, since White can reply at C. Keep your options open.

5

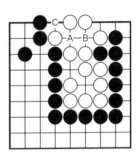

6

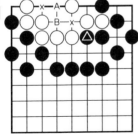

White's territory is in a shape normally worth two eyes. White can play at either A or B to separate the two x points. The territory is not quite solidly surrounded though, and the marked black stone makes a tiny weakness which can be exploited to spoil one of the eyes.

HINTS FOR PROBLEMS 7–12

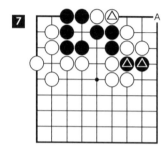

Capturing two stones at the top threatens an eye, but White can throw in a stone at the marked point and steal it unless the capture is also atari on something else. Black also has room for an eye at A. Combining these two possibilities with perfect timing is just enough.

Maximizing the space by capturing at A would allow white D, leaving only one eye's worth. There are only four interesting places to play, and one of them works. Don't abandon any variation until you are sure you have reached the end of it.

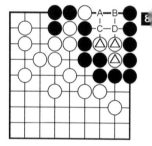

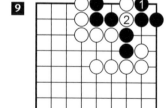

There is absolutely no choice about black 1. If White plays here the space inside the group will surely only be worth one eye. But then White is going to start sacrifice manoeuvres with 2, hoping to end up leaving a false eye at 2. What can Black do to prevent this from working?

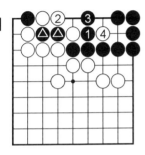

Black has no way to save the two marked stones, but threatening to save them with 1 leaves White able to prevent two eyes at either 3 or 4. Black has to find a way to make more use of the dead stones to the left.

There is no room for two eyes in the corner. Black A gets white B and vice versa. So Black had better find some way to do damage to the marked white stone. Persistence is required here.

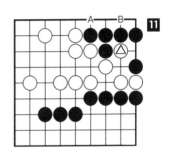

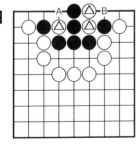

Black can make an eye by capturing one stone with A, and can make another eye by capturing two stones with B. But two eyes are required to live. Black needs to find a way to make one eye that requires an answer, so that there is time to make the other one as well.

CHAPTER TEN:
CULTURE OF GO

There is no reliable history of the origins of Go. There is a popular myth that it was invented by the Emperor Yao around 2250 BC as an exercise for his son, and this was widely accepted through the Far East for several millennia. Modern historians find most aspects of this account to be highly implausible.

William Pinckard, a student of Chinese history and philosophy argues that the most likely origin of the game was as one of the tools used for divination by the shaman-astrologers of the early Chou culture, somewhere between 1300 and 900 BC. The best known of these tools is the I Ching, but there were a number of other systems used at that time. One method is thought to have involved the casting of black and white counters onto a square board marked with symbols.

This suggestion for the origin of the game at least accounts for the existence of something quite close to suitable equipment for playing Go, and among a class of people used to cerebral activity.

It is certain that the game was already an established part of Chinese culture well before the birth of Christ. Its modern Chinese name, Wei Chi – "surrounding pieces" – first appears around the third century AD. Its popularity among the classes with sufficient leisure to play games varied greatly. Of the two main threads in Chinese thinking, the game was less favoured by the Confucians, whose outlook was more rationalist and mechanical, and more by the Taoists. Their holistic approach saw much of life as a voyage of self-discovery.

The emperors of the T'ang dynasty (618–906 AD) leaned strongly towards the Taoist way of thinking, and it was during this period that there was vigorous commerce with Korea and Japan. The popularity of the game in court circles seems to have extended to travelling government officials, and the game spread through them to the Koreans and the Japanese.

THE SPREAD TO JAPAN

Cultural contact between Japan and China can be dated to an ambassador sent from Japan in 607 AD. It is likely that some knowledge of the game of Go arrived in Japan soon after that time. Actual mentions of the game in Japanese accounts start with the return from China of an ambassador called Kibi in 740 AD. This was a period when the game was particularly popular in Chinese court circles. It is likely that reports of its popularity among influential people would have excited more interest than mere accounts of the existence of the game.

It was during the eighth century that Go became popular among court circles in Japan, and it soon spread to the Samurai (warrior) classes. By the time that the Tale of Genji was written in the 11th century, it seems to have become an established part of Japanese cultural life.

The actual game being played during this period was very similar to that played today, but it differed in one important respect. Rather than starting with the board empty, four stones were placed as shown in the diagram. The effect of this pattern was to prevent either side from developing a really large sphere of influence, so that the game usually became fragmented into small areas early on. Starting with the same point in each corner also made for rather stereotyped opening play.

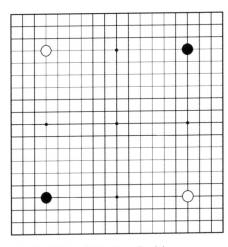

The Traditional Starting Position

JAPANESE MONKS AND SHOGUNS

Go was widely played among the educated classes in Japan from the eighth century. The most skillful players belonged mainly to the Buddhist clergy, especially those of the Nichiren sect, named from its founder who lived in the 13th century.

Japanese culture puts a particularly strong emphasis on respecting ones forbears, and it is common that the founder of a school of thought should be attributed with developments which did not really occur until several generations later. A similar situation occurs in Western philosophy, where Plato is personally credited with several hundred years' worth of work by his successors. This makes it difficult to know how much influence Nichiren actually had on the developments in Go theory which were made by monks of his school.

There is a game record, dated 1253, which purports to be of a game played by Nichiren. It is widely believed to be a forgery, but whatever the names of the key players, it is clear that Nichiren monks were among the best Go players through the next four hundred years.

Some time during this period a key development took place – the abandonment of the four fixed stones at the start of the game. This opened the door for a great leap in understanding of the possibilities of the game, and it was the first important development in moving the Japanese game to new levels of skill well beyond those they had inherited from the Chinese. The fixed opening stones were not abandoned in China until the 1920s.

The next major leap forward came with the establishment of a government grant to what were effectively professional players. A key figure in this process was the warlord Oda Nobunaga, who was assassinated in 1582. Nobunaga was a keen Go player, and employed the best player of his day, a Nichiren monk named Nikkai, as his teacher. Nobunaga's successor Toyotomi Hideyoshi was also keen on Go, and organized a tournament among the leading players of the day in 1588. Nikkai was awarded an annual income when he won this event. Nikkai continued to outlive his mentors, and when Japan was unified under Tokugawa Ieyasu, he was brought out of retirement in 1603 as the head of a new government office dedicated to the development of Go.

The structure set up by this office continued to the end of the 19th century, with four separate Go schools set up as rivals to each other and a formal ranking system which was controlled centrally. If there was one player who was clearly stronger than any of his rivals, this player was titled Meijin (brilliant man) and became eligible to be the head of the government office. For much of the period though there was no one player far enough ahead to merit this title, and important decisions were made by a commitee of the heads of the four Go houses.

The main competition at which the rival houses established their relative strengths was the annual Castle game ceremony. In principle, this consisted of games played in the presence of the shogun, but normally the games were actually played a few days beforehand, and then replayed at a much faster rate for the shogun's benefit. Of the four schools, the Honinbo group – named from the temple at which Nikkai had been a monk – was by far the most successful over the years. Two figures in particular stand out in history.

Dosaku (1645–1702) is popularly regarded as the strongest Go player ever. He was certainly well ahead of any of his contemporaries, and his developments in opening theory and in analysis of the efficiency of stones provided most of the important ideas for the next 200 years' developments. Shusaku (1829–1862) had the benefit of a much stronger group of contemporaries than Dosaku, but he had established a lead over all of them before his early death from cholera. He is best known for winning all 17 of his castle games, and his games are still required study material for aspiring professionals.

CHAPTER 10

THE 20TH CENTURY

J apanese politics had been relatively stable through the period of the four Go houses, with rigid central control from Edo (Tokyo) and a deliberate policy of isolation from the rest of the world. When the frontiers were opened again in the late 19th century, the opportunity arose for the formidable body of expertize in Go playing to spread to other countries.

But within Japan, political instability led to the reduction of government grants to Go professionals. The game did not regain its former support until the economic recovery after the second world war, though there had been some outstanding players active in the 1930s who made the first really significant advances in the theory of the game since Dosaku's time.

One of these players, Kitani Minoru (1909–1975), founded a highly successful Go school whose pupils continue to dominate the professional scene in Japan. The 50 or so resident students in his house typically began serious study of the game before the age of 10, and those destined for success were already top level players in their teens. This sort of intensive dedication to the game has become unpopular in Japan over the last 15 years or so. The generation of players trained by Kitani has surprisingly few obvious successors.

A strong challenge to Japanese supremacy comes from South Korea, where the largest and keenest amateur following in the world supports a professional Go community which includes several very promising young players. The most outstanding of these, Lee Changho, was born in 1975 and has ceased to be "promising". He is arguably the world's strongest player. An astonishingly rapid revival of the game in China – starting when a prohibition on playing it was lifted at the end of the cultural revolution – has also produced another serious rival to Japanese supremacy in the game.

At the time of writing, the top Chinese players are no stronger than the best Japanese ones. Most of them are 20 years younger however, and although most Go players retain their peak strength into their 50s it seems unlikely that Japan can hold its position for long.

THE GAME SPREADS TO EUROPE

When Japan opened its frontiers to international contact in the 1860s, the strongest links in Europe were with Germany. A Go teacher was sent to Europe to introduce the game, and a small but dedicated group of players has been active in Berlin ever since. The game spread to a few other cities, notably Vienna, and a separate group was formed in the 1920s by a Yugoslav naval officer in Ljubljana.

The progress of all of these groups was restricted by the lack of books on the game. A few publications in German and English, along with the inclusion of Go in some general books on games, slowly began to bring the game to a wider public.

Go was still restricted to a very small group of dedicated games enthusiasts until business contacts between Europe and the far East started to develop in the 1950s. Travellers to Japan brought back their enthusiasm for the game, and associations were formed in Britain, France and Holland during this period. An enormous boost to the standard of Go playing came about in the late 1960s, when two Western expatriates living in Japan started to produce a series of high-class Go books in English. These brought access to much of the accumulated wisdom of centuries of Japanese study to the West for the first time.

There is only so much that can be done from books though, and the required opportunities to play against experienced Eastern players began to appear during the 1980s. The steady expansion of the Oriental business community in Europe has provided important contacts, but much the most important development was the institution in 1980 of the Amateur World Championship. At first this was mainly an Eastern affair, with a small number of Western players to provide an international flavour, but the Eastern nations were soon reduced to one representative each. The number of countries competing has increased steadily, approaching 50 as the millennium approaches.

HANDICAPS AND RANKING

As in most sports, players of Go are measured according to a numerical ranking. Ranks in Go play a much larger part than in many other games, since there is an effective handicapping system which enables players of widely differing ability to compete on more or less equal terms.

The handicap system is very simple. The player with the black stones (Black always plays first in Go) is allowed a fixed number of extra moves at the start of the game. The system most widely used around the world is for these extra stones to be placed on the star points (the little dots, on the centre spot and on the fourth line) in a prescribed order. But in China – and some other areas – the handicap stones may be played wherever Black likes.

When fixed handicap points are used, it is not normal to give more than 9 stones handicap. The fixed patterns are shown on the next page. The centre spot is included in the handicap for 5, 7 and 9 stones, otherwise the stones are placed symmetrically, leaving Black's upper left corner until last. If the handicap is one stone, Black just plays first, and is always free to choose where.

The standard (Japanese) ranking system for amateurs makes a difference of one grade between players represent a handicap of one stone at the beginning of the game. It turns out that the difference between a complete beginner with a few games' experience and a top expert is about 45 grades. The ranks are measured from first Dan, which is about 10 grades below the top professional level. Stronger players than this are ranked from second Dan up to the strongest amateur level at seventh Dan, and weaker players are ranked downwards from first Kyu, which is one grade below first Dan, to about 35th Kyu, which is a beginner's level.

Professional grades are awarded separately, and on a different scale. They rank from Professional First Dan, which is actually a somewhat higher

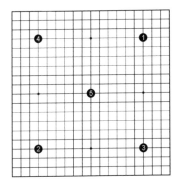
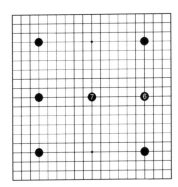

Where to place the handicap stones

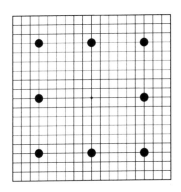
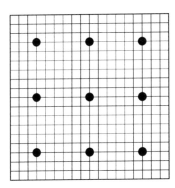

level then most amateur seventh Dan players, up to ninth Dan. These grades are much closer together than amateur grades, and a professional first Dan player would expect to beat the top players taking three stones' handicap.

The awarding of professional Dan certificates is done by professional associations, which exist in Japan, South Korea, China and Taiwan.

PROFESSIONAL ASSOCIATIONS

The largest body of professional players is in Japan, with over 300 players. There are approximately 100 in each of South Korea and the Republic of China, and a smaller group in Taiwan. These players are supported by their national associations, which derive income from television and newspaper sponsorship as well as the sale of books and magazines. In addition to their salaries as members of the professional associations, the players earn money from teaching the game in various ways and get prize money for playing in sponsored tournaments. The top players in Japan and Korea can earn around $1 million in a year, but to do this you have to win a lot of games. The majority of the professional community command no more than a comfortable salary.

Within the Western Go community, there are so few opportunities to make money by playing the game that even the best players can only earn a living by emigrating to the far East. But the organisation of the game is expanding to become too large a job for voluntary workers to cope with reasonably, and in several of the more active countries a few very hard-working volunteers are looking for ways to make at least a part-time living from their favourite game.

The foundation of the European Go and Cultural Centre in Amsterdam in 1992 was an important landmark in this quest. Financed initially from Japan, a staff of four is now supported by a range of games activities, but they devote most of their time to the spreading of Go around Europe.

Meanwhile, in North America, a somewhat different Go community has grown up. The rather larger number of expatriate Orientals in America, especially on the West Coast, means there are several Go players who were formerly professionals in the far East. Recently a North American professional Guild has been formed, with eight members, most of whom earn their living by teaching the game within the United States.

THE FUTURE

Most of the Go-playing community outside the far East still consists of players who learned the game as adults. The arrival of a second generation who have known the game from childhood will undoubtedly cause a further improvement in the level of play and boost the extent to which the game is a part of the normal run of cultural activity. Meanwhile the continued growth of semi-professional organizing bodies will help to bring the game to a wider audience.

In terms of the actual way the game is played, the most interesting development in recent years is the invention of "Pair Go", in which four players take part. Each side consists of one player of each sex, playing alternate moves with no consultation. There is a very active body in Japan promoting this version of the game, and a sponsored world championship held each year provides opportunities for players from around the world to travel to Japan and meet other players. This form of Go tends to be more sociable than most thinking games, and apart from the opportunity to travel and meet people it brings other advantages. Playing occasional games with two players on one side allows a small Go club to find games for everyone when an odd number of players are present. The possibility to have evenly-matched games between players of widely-differing ability is expanded enormously by pairing the strongest player present with the weakest. This is also an excellent forum for learning about the game from your partner.

A possibility which is being canvassed strongly in some quarters is to have Go included as an Olympic sport. This requires the presence of formally constituted organizing bodies in at least 50 countries, which is roughly the number with active playing communities at present.

The spread of the game in some form seems guaranteed. The monopoly of top players that Japan has enjoyed for the last thousand years is brittle at best. Where the centre of activity will move to next is hard to guess, though.

CHAPTER 10

COMPUTERS AND GO

Gary Kasparov's recent difficulty in handling computer opponents has been described as the fall of the last citadel in the battle of humans against the encroaching computer menace, but Go still stands as a refuge well beyond the reach of current programmers. This is not for want of trying. The late Ing Chiang Ki from Taiwan sponsored an annual Go tournament for computers with good prize money, and several of the entrants put in years of work on their programs. But the tournament finishes with a challenge match between the winner and a teenage human. This has to be played with a huge handicap – currently 14 free moves at the start of the game – and this is only diminishing slowly.

Part of the reason for this is accidental. Although for a human brain Chess and Go present similar challenges, there is an easy way to see how well you are doing at Chess – just count the pieces on the board. Looking a few moves ahead and counting the balance of pieces which results gives a quick and easy way to avoid silly moves. Chess computers only need to be clever at sorting out a small number of "sensible" alternatives.

There is no such simple method in Go. Positions do not have a clear value until the game is finished, and the same pattern of stones may work perfectly in one context and be almost worthless in another. One source of the great strategic richness of Go is that you can choose between making large-scale loose formations and small-scale solid ones and each provides for different types of efficient development.

There are certain types of localized position in which computers have been used to find the right moves by exhaustive analysis, but even for quite modest-sized problems the programs run into millions of variations. This is simply not a practical approach to most Go positions. It comes as something of a relief to discover that methodical calculation, considering all the possible outcomes, is neither necessary nor very useful in Go.

How are people able to play Go so well, then? Much of the answer lies in the incredible ability of the human eye to recognize and sort patterns. Go is a very visual game, and much of the process of becoming proficient at the game involves training your eye to find suitable moves without requiring much analysis.

Imagine that you have followed a footpath through a wood, not really trying to remember the way since the path was easy to see. Some years afterwards you return, but now it is winter and the path is obscured by snow. If you try to analyse your memory of the route you will probably have no idea where you are, but if you just relax and keep walking, your eye can assemble enough clues to find the way. This fantastic ability is present in most people, and Go provides a stimulating way for this skill to get out and exercise itself.

The science of writing computer programs which can recognize patterns is, by contrast, at a very early stage. The relatively simple problem of reading handwritten addresses on envelopes has taken many years and many millions of pounds. It still does not work very well, despite the limited nature of the problem. There are only 26 letters to distinguish, and there is a pretty good idea of what kind of word they are trying to form. In a typical Go position, the stones should form themselves into groups with a common purpose in your mind long before they actually connect solidly along the lines. The question of what kind of pattern it is reasonable to look for is much less clear.

The human ability to switch scale rapidly – looking at small details while keeping broad objectives in mind, and using each of those things to direct the attention of the other – is another well-developed trick which computers have not yet been taught effectively.

In short, the game of Go includes several of the most challenging and exciting problems which computer programmers are just beginning to tackle, and it also provides an opportunity to let your brain do the things it is best at. The mechanical calculating part of your brain can only gape in awe at the fountain of rich imagination which pours from the intuitive part when you let it out.

FINDING OPPONENTS

Many European countries now have formal Go associations, and there are clubs meeting regularly in nearly all of the large cities. These are by no means restricted to players with long experience of the game. The effective handicapping system means that even a complete beginner can find suitable opponents among much more experienced players.

Most clubs meet once a week, but a few of the larger ones are open every day, especially those based on cafes and social clubs. Some addresses are given in the list of references on page 125, or if you have access to the Internet there are several web pages with address lists to help you find the others.

If your national association is unable to find a group of other players near your home, there is the alternative of playing Go through the Internet. There are several sites supporting Go in real time across the world by this method. It is particularly suitable for players in very remote areas and for insomniacs, who can easily find someone elsewhere in the world who is awake at what is for them a reasonable time. At most times of day there are 100 or so games in progress, and you have the option of watching – or, alternatively, discussing – other people's games in progress as well as playing your own.

If you are interested in combining games with travel, there are tournaments somewhere in Europe almost every weekend. During the summer, there are a number of longer events, lasting one or two weeks. These provide an opportunity to meet a range of players at different levels, and also give you the kind of contact with locals that allows a much more involved form of tourism than simply looking at places and staying in hotels. The Go-playing community is still small enough that new players are welcomed everywhere as new friends. This is perhaps one of the best reasons for becoming involved with the game.

CONTACT ADDRESSES

BRITISH GO ASSOCIATION
37 Courts Road, Earley, Reading, RG6 7DG. http://www.britgo.demon.co.uk/

EUROPEAN GO CENTRE
Schokland 14, 1181 HV Amstelveen, Nederlands Tel +20 645 5555

FRENCH GO ASSOCIATION
75262 Paris Cedex 06, France

GERMAN GO ASSOCIATION
Postfach 60 54 54, neu: 22249 Hamburg, Deutschland

USA
PO Box 397, Old Chelsea Station, New York, NY 10113 0397, USA

JAPAN
Nihon Kiin, 7-2 Goban cho Chiyoda Ku, Tokyo, Japan

CANADA
D. Erbach, 71 Brixford Crescent, Winnipeg, Manitoba R2N1E1, Canada.

SOUTH AFRICAN GO ASSOCIATION
PO Box 561, Parklands, Johannesburg, 2121 RSA

NEW ZEALAND
M. Taler, 76 Marsden Ave, Auckland, New Zealand

AUSTRALIA
GPO Box 65, Canberra ACT, Australia 2601

FURTHER READING

Much the best way to develop your Go is to play a lot of games. But if you only have other inexperienced players to play against, there are many features of the game which will take a long time to discover. The most effective way to improve your standard at first will be to learn a lot of tactical tricks. This can be done by working through collections of problems, of which the most suitable is:

Graded Problems for Beginners (4 volumes) by Kano Yoshinori, translated from the Japanese. The first two of these volumes are suitable for beginners. Published by the Nihon Kiin (Japanese Go Association), ISBN 8182-0228-2 C2376.

The first batch of English language books produced in Japan include some of the best introductions to many areas of the game. The whole range of tactical tricks is introduced in *Tesuji* by James Davies, Ishi Press (Japan) 1975, recently reprinted. The essentials of opening theory are described by the same author in *In The Beginning*, ISBN 4-87187-010-4.

For those who prefer a racier style with a transatlantic flavour, a good general survey of the game is *EZ Go, Oriental Strategy in a Nutshell* by Bruce and Sue Wilcox, Ki Press 1996, ISBN 0-9652235-4-X.

THE WORLD WIDE WEB

FEEDBACK

If you would like to discuss anything in this book, discover what other people think about it, or see the answers to the Challenge problems, visit the author's web page: http://www.jklmn.demon.co.uk/Carlton

This site will be kept up to date with your comments and answers to them.

THE INTERNET

There is a large amount of information about Go on the Internet, and once you start browsing, most of the larger sites have a good range of pointers to the others. A good place to start is the British Go Association's page: http://www.britgo.demon.co.uk/

The largest collection of references is kept by Ken Warkentyne: http://nngs.cosmic.org/hmkw/golinks.html

The most thorough discussion of the rules of the game and the effects of small variations in them is at: http://www.snafu.de/~jasiek/

The European Go centre can be found at: http:www.xs4all.nl/~egcc/

The American Go Association is at: http://www.usgo.org

A site for playing Go over the Internet is: http://www.igs.nuri.net/

General chit-chat and other info on the game can be found on the newsgroup rec.games.go

INDEX